Rum Drinks
50 Caribbean Cocktails, from Cuba Libre to Rum Daisy

Rum Drinks

50 Caribbean Cocktails, from Cuba Libre to Rum Daisy

by **Jessica B. Harris**

photographs by Tara Donne

CHRONICLE BOOKS
SAN FRANCISCO

Library of Congress Cataloging-in-Publication
Data available.

ISBN 978-0-8118-6699-6

Manufactured in China.

Designed by Brooke Johnson
Prop styling by Lili Diallo
Food styling by Liza Jernow
Typesetting by Janis Reed
The photographer wishes to thank Andrew Camp.
Vintage photographs and ephemera from the
collection of Jessica B. Harris.

The consumption of raw eggs is not recommended
for those who have compromised immune systems.

10 9 8 7 6 5 4 3 2 1

Chronicle Books LLC
680 Second Street
San Francisco, California 94107
www.chroniclebooks.com

I pour three splashes of *clairin* on the ground and dedicate this book to the ancestors, to my parents, and to the members of my personal "bar association" with whom I've sampled more than one taste of the history in a glass that is rum.

ACHE

Contents

chapter 1

Rum: History in a Glass

The flowers were still blooming on

Papa Doc's tomb and the eternal flame was flickering in the torrid wind the first time I tasted rum. I'd arrived in Port au Prince, Haiti, the previous evening and been whisked off to that gingerbread hotel, the legendary Oloffson, celebrated by Graham Greene in *The Comedians*. The hotel was every writer's dream—with the flotsam and jetsam of the island circulating at cocktail time. Modern-day pirates rubbed shoulders with pale-skinned newcomers, their sharp eyes evaluating the worth of each summer cotton frock and gold-braceleted arm and calculating schemes and scams. Paint-daubed artists sought solace in the bottom of glasses, weary island-exiled writers fled from the blank page, socialites fought ennui, and white linen–suited Aubelin Jolicoeur, the model for Greene's character Petitpierre, hovered: a celebrity in search of an audience. The sophistication was palpable.

With the hindsight of three decades, it seems somehow fitting that there, at the mahogany bar in the main room under the whirling ceiling fans, I had my first taste of Rhum Barbancourt—the first rum that I sipped in the Caribbean. Served in a snifter, the beverage was the color of good Georgian amber and it flickered in the glass. The taste, a combination of caramel and molasses, was deceptively light and the intense aroma of the alcohol would soon reveal that this was a drink to savor and sip.

No matter where you had your first Caribbean cocktail, whether it came in a coconut freshly lopped off the tree or in a frosted glass of etched Waterford, the sweet molasses flavor of rum was more than likely an ingredient. The memory may have faded, but the taste of rum will forever conjure up warm breezes, fluttering palm fronds, lilting bawdy calypsos, haunting *bigines*, deep turquoise sea, and romance.

I had my first Caribbean cocktail back in the days when every island's airport welcome came complete with a plastic cup of something pinkish-orange, rum-infused, and wonderful enough to make even the most crotchety tourist forget the travails of baggage claim and hotel check-in. The concoction was never truly memorable—but it was always strong—and it signaled one's arrival into a universe of cocktails that were and are legendary.

Since those halcyon days, I have traveled the Caribbean region through and through. I've sampled superb piña coladas at their alleged birthplace in Viejo San Juan in Puerto Rico, and savored how they can truly be transformed into the sublime when prepared from freshly made coconut cream, chopped fresh pineapple, and aged rum and served in a coconut shell on a pristine beach. I've become an honorary member of more than one of the region's "bar associations" and indulged in my share and more of the drink called "Corn and Oil" (rum and *falernum*) with locals at Letzie's in Christ Church, Barbados, the island where rum began its Caribbean journey. I've visited Hemingway's Cuban spots and had a daiquiri or two at La Floridita and mojitos at La Bodeguita del Medio way before they turned up in pallid versions on almost every bar menu, back when travel to Cuba was legal for a few brief minutes under President Carter. I've stood on the lawn of Rose Hall in the evening amidst ghosts from the Jamaica's plantation past while sipping a version of rum punch that harked back to those days. I savor the *rhum agricole* of the French islands since I learned to correctly dose out my white rum, sugar, and lime juice to make a 'ti punch and to create my own passion fruit–flavored *rhum arrangés*.

I've visited rum factories too numerous to note and been stuck behind cane trucks bringing the harvest home. I've learned to recognize the parallel row of palm trees that usually signal the placement of a former sugar estate, and know the smell of burning *bagasse* (cane waste). I've watched the cane growing cycle of tiny green shoots peeking from the rich chocolaty soil to the feathery flowers that signal the approach of harvest. I've judged bartending competitions and savored snifters from the Bahamas to Venezuela and I've even seen the green flash . . . twice! I remain intoxicated not only by the beverage, but by the history that is contained in each amber glassful.

Rum History

Before there was rum there was sugar. Man has long evidenced a yearning for the sweet. This taste has been satisfied by sweeteners ranging from the maple syrup of the northeastern United States to the bee's honey around the world. None, though, have attained the international primacy of cane sugar and its by-product, rum. Sugar from cane is so much a part of our lives now that we take it for granted. One has only to go into the nearest deli or Starbuck's to note the abandon with which we use the little white and brown packets, and the prices in the supermarket attest to the fact that this commodity is no longer considered scarce. We consume a staggering 66 to 88 pounds of sugars and syrups per capita in the United States and are still considered slackers when compared to the upward of 100 pounds that are the norm in countries like Australia, Brazil, and Fiji, and the 120 pounds-plus currently ingested in Cuba. (Statisticians don't tell whether these figures include rum drinking; if so, the figures become a bit more understandable.)

Sugar gets taken for granted, but it is very much a part of who we are in the Americas, and its presence explains why some of us are here at all. Rum is a major New World part of the story of sugar, a story that is strung across hemispheres and borders. The powdery white substance was once as rare and as controlled as others like cocaine and heroin are today and its evolution and history equal the most circuitous of drug routes. Its by-product—rum—lubricates every aspect of our history.

GUADELOUPE. - Chauds partisans de la canne à sucre
Édit. Phos, Pointe-à-Pître (Guadeloupe)

RHUM PUR

R.C.C. 10212

CANE-HOLEING.

Sugarcane looks very much like any other grass in the savanna. Some variants of it still grow wild in the tropical fields of New Guinea. Tall and segmented like bamboo, with its reed-like stalk filled with sweet sap, *Saccharum robustum* is at the origin of the main cultivated sugarcane species we know today. Cane has been recognized for at least 2,200 years and is a curiously adaptable plant. A perennial with a deep root system, cane can flourish and grow upward of fifteen feet tall. It requires little water, but will do well when properly irrigated. It is tolerant of a wide range of soil conditions and can grow on both hillsides and flat land.

No one knows whether by man, weather, or spontaneous generation that cane migrated, but cane was growing in India and possibly China early in written history. It is in India, though, where the sugar-bearing reed gained importance. There its modern story began, and it became one of the first plants to inspire man to technology. Instead of chewing it to release its sweet juice, cane farmers learned they could concentrate the sweetness of the plant by crushing and boiling the cane. Sugar-cane presses were used to grind the stalks just like oil presses. Early Indian texts suggest that the cane was transformed into many different types of sugar with special medicinal effects attributed to each. There was no rum in India, but there were a variety of medicinal beverages and a drink called *samyava*—a blend of wheat flour, milk, ghee, and sugar flavored with cardamom, pepper, and ginger. Rock sugar called *khand* (from whence our word candy comes) was first described in Western texts in 326 or 327 BCE by those in the retinue of Alexander

DE L'AMERIQUE. 327

FIGURE CXLIII.

SVCRERIE

the Great as, "stones the color of frankincense, sweeter than figs or honey."

Alexander the Great's armies may have seen sugar on the subcontinent, but sugarcane's voyage to Europe and from there to the New World was a slow one and its subsequent transmutation into rum would take more than a millennium. Unlike chiles, which swept around the world in less than a century, cane took 700 years to make its way from Southern Asia to the shores of the Mediterranean and an additional 700 more to make its way across the Atlantic.

Texts on sugar and its journey can fill a library row or two; those on rum scarcely fill one shelf. It seems no one is sure of the origins of rum. The drink may have originated in Europe or even in the Middle East or on the Indian sub-continent itself. The trail is, quite simply, cold. Sugarcane was brought to the Caribbean by Columbus in 1493; his diaries remark on the abundance of the harvest, but it seems that there was no attempt made to cultivate it on a large scale and no real record as to whether or not the Admiral of the Seas and his men made any attempt to distill the cane into a beverage of any kind.

Kill Devil's Conquest

Rum turns up for the first time in the glasses of the New World as reported by an English adventurer named Ligon. Richard Ligon was an informed voyager and the most valuable of travelers: an observer and a chronicler. His thoughts on the new land of Barbados were published in a volume entitled *A True & Exact History of the Island of Barbadoes*.

He describes the island, draws the earliest surviving map on which he notes 285 plantations and their owners, and details life of all the inhabitants from the plantocracy to the enslaved Africans. Ligon's skills as a cartographer aside, he deserves to be revered by historians and rum drinkers everywhere, as he is the first Englishman to describe the beverage called Kill-Devil that would be known as rum three years later.

The sugar that Ligon and those like him went to Barbados to cultivate made the fortunes of more than one Englishman and the expression "As rich as a Barbados planter" came to symbolize the excesses of wealth that Internet moguls and stock market masters of the universe have come to represent today. Sugar was king, and rum and rum drinking defined that world.

In the decades of the sugar boom, Barbados was a world where the classical order of things was turned topsy-turvy. Hard liquor was a fact of daily life among all classes, from the aristocracy who began their day with *flips* and *cobblers* and beakers of *shrub*, to the enslaved who drank themselves insensate when they could on rough unrefined rum. Drinking establishments known as tippling houses were everywhere. They outnumbered churches two to one, and the tiny island boasted one for every twenty inhabitants. It is estimated that Barbadians in the seventeenth century consumed ten gallons of rum annually—no small feat given that it was an oily and unrefined beverage then. It fit the times though, for it was a world that required a little muting around the edges.

Rich as a Barbados Planter

Barbados, in all of its bilious excess, was the crucible in which the sugar culture of the Caribbean islands was formed. With help from the Dutch from Pernambuco in northeastern Brazil, Barbadian planters learned the technology of mass-producing sugar in great enough quantities to undercut the monopolies held by sugar producers from the Mediterranean and the Canary Islands. More important, they discovered that they could process the molasses waste from sugar production into rum, which could then be sold to offset production costs so that their sugar revenues represented clear profit! Slave labor from the African continent and the labor-intensive plantation system rendered sugar an unbeatable business venture. Soon, second sons and adventurers looking to make their fortunes sought out every island in the region that could plant enough acreage of cane and support crushing mills and boiling houses. In 1764, Scotsman James Grainger penned a four-book poem "The Sugar Cane" celebrating the plant, in which he extolled, quite lengthily indeed, its virtues enjoining planters:

> While flows the juice mellifluent from the Cane,
> Grudge not, my friend, to let thy slaves, each morn,
> But chief the sick and young at setting day,
> Themselves regale with oft-repeated draughts
> Of tepid Nectar; so shall health and strength

Confirm thy Negroes, and make labor light.

Grainger wrote of the sugar plantations on the island of St. Kitts. As the plantation system became more firmly embedded, settlers were transformed into colonizers throughout the region. The small Caribbean islands combined produced and sent more wealth to the European mother countries than did the entire region of the northern colonies that would become the United States. The culture of imbibing rum grew and flourished. Plantation hospitality became the norm and centered on vast consumption of alcohol, including the many concoctions prepared from rum that remain hallmarks of the region's bars. The planter's punches and rum punches and cobblers and flips remain living history, and the welcome drinks that are served in many a Caribbean hotel hark back to traditions of hospitality that were established in this period. The fruity creations served to mute some of the fire of the rum then, and made the drinks more genteel. Punches were particular favorites.

In fact, punch has been called the first international beverage and turns up on the Indian subcontinent and in the Caribbean as well as in England and throughout the nascent United States. The name seems to come from the Persian *panj* or the Hindi word *panch*, meaning "five." *A Glossary of Colloquial Anglo-Indian Words and Phrases* (also referred to as Hobson-Jobson), gives a three-column definition of the word, but suggests that the original beverage may have been prepared from five ingredients: *arrack* (palm liquor), sugar, lime

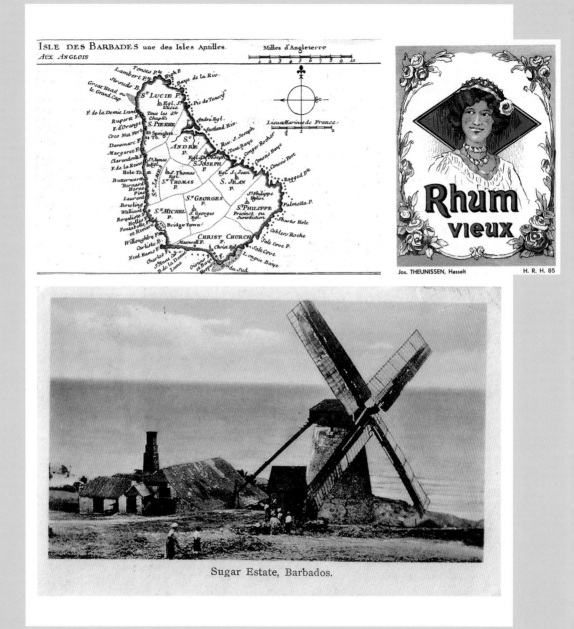

Sugar Estate, Barbados.

juice, spice, and water. In the Caribbean the tipple was rum, and so the Caribbean punch was born. Rivers of it were consumed at parties and on at least one occasion, a lake of it:

A marble basin, built in the middle of the garden especially for the occasion, served as a bowl. Into it were poured 1,200 bottles of rum, 1,200 bottles of Malaga wine, and 400 quarts of boiling water. Then 600 pounds of the best cane sugar and 200 powdered nutmegs were added. The juice of 2,600 lemons was squeezed into the liquor. Onto the surface was launched a handsome mahogany boat piloted by a boy of twelve who rowed about a few moments, then coasted to the side and began to serve the assembled company of 600, which gradually drank up the ocean upon which he floated.

Back in the colonial period, Barbadian plantation owners—who were the *nouveau riche* of the period—really knew how to throw a party! After seriously imbibing during the festivities, drink-loving colonists would cap off the evening with a nightcap of still more rum. It's a miracle more of them didn't succumb to alcohol-related ailments.

Molasses to Rum to Slaves
However, all was not punches and *sangaree*. For more than three centuries, rum fueled the trans-Atlantic slave trade. Barrels of it were exchanged for human cargo in the ports of Western and Central Africa. The drink became

so popular as a means of trade that by the late eighteenth century, rum had replaced French brandy as a means of exchange all up and down the West African Coast. Rhode Island broke the French monopoly by annually carrying the equivalent of 113,000 gallons of rum to Africa for the period between 1740 and 1760. Caribbean molasses was shipped to the American colonies, where it was transformed into Guinea rum, an especially distilled variant that was concentrated for shipping and had to be watered down upon arrival on the African coast. In 1767, the standard slave price at Cape Coast Castle on the Gold Coast (present day Ghana) was 130 gallons per man, 110 per woman, and 80 per girl. By 1770, the price had risen to 210 to 220 gallons per slave.

In the Caribbean islands where cane was the sole agricultural product, sugar provided a reason for toil for enslaved Africans, while rum often offered a release from it. The French Code Noir specifically forbade planters from working their slaves on rum alone. Yet rum was a daily constant from the boiling houses to the Big House and all consumed. The trading of rum and slaves ultimately made sugar and its by-product beverage targets of abolitionist's ire in the late eighteenth century, as much of the Atlantic world began to move toward the abolition of the slave trade.

Yo Ho Ho and a Bottle of Rum

Slavers and slave ships were not the only vessels connected with rum. For centuries the beverage lubricated sailing men, be they privateers or Jack Tars. It seems that once the drink was created, among the first to take it to heart were those who sailed. From the early days of Caribbean settlement, the navies of Europe continued that continent's conflicts and skirmishes on the other side of the Atlantic. All of the islands, with the exception of Barbados—which has remained resolutely British since 1627—exchanged conquering hands at least once and some of them multiple times. On some Caribbean islands, it strains all but the true maritime history buff to keep track of the treaties and turnovers. Pirates, buccaneers, and privateers ruled the waves long before Britannia.

Pirates have been a part of the world of the sea since man first set out on the water, but the Caribbean region transformed the turquoise seas into a battleground for supremacy. The images that we have of gold doubloons and pieces of eight and Johnny Depp–like characters saying "arrgh" are false. In truth the pirates of the Caribbean were originally licensed by the English crown to harass the Spaniards who had strongholds in the region, given "letters of marque and reprisal" that specified the types of vessels that they could harass, and considered to be a legitimate arm of government. Sir Francis Drake and John Hawkins were pirates of this type in the sixteenth century and Sir Henry Morgan and Captain Kidd in the seventeenth. Soon enough, the system broke down and piracy became the rule of the day, with bands of the so-called "brethren of the coast" having strongholds on the island of Tortuga north of Haiti and in the city of Port Royal, Jamaica—the virtual pirate capital, reputed to be the wickedest city in the world. Tales of drunken debauches and fights started in the heat of inebriation were the norm.

Smiling grog is the sailor's best hope, his sheet anchor,
His compass, his cable, his log.
That gives him a heart which life's care cannot canker,
Though dangers around him
Unite to confound him,
He braves them and tips off his grog.
'Tis grog, only grog,
Is his rudder, his compass, his cable, his log,
The sailor's best anchor is grog.

Charles Dibdin (1745–1814)

Serving out Rum

Rule Britannia

Legitimate navies were the other side of the nautical picture. British statesman Sir Winston Churchill, an army man himself, once dismissed British naval traditions as "rum, sodomy, and the lash." The last two are overstated, but it is undeniable that rum was one of the pillars of service. The crews of sailing ships were notoriously rough, and Samuel Johnson opined that he'd rather go to prison than to sea because he'd not have to worry about drowning and he'd meet a better class of folk. In fact, he might have met many of the same folk because the necessities of manning a large navy meant that often the crews were either shanghaied lowlifes, prisoners serving their sentences in forced labor, or hapless locals who had been press-ganged into active service. Hard life at sea, with brutal discipline by floggings for the slightest infraction of the rules, made alcohol a rule of service. Beer was the original drink, but in 1655, during the Jamaican campaign, Vice Admiral William Penn distributed a rum ration to his sailors and it rapidly became the official beverage of the Royal Navy. The ration was a half pint per day, which the sailors drank neat in one gulp, usually before lunch on an empty stomach with predictable results. Reports of sailors too drunk to climb the ships' ropes abound, and where the rare shore leaves were granted, the resulting chaos was equally predictable.

When Edward Vernon, an eighteenth-century vice admiral of the British fleet and commander in chief in the West Indies, noticed that inebriation among sailors was causing more than the usual number of accidents, he issued a general order to his captains that the daily ration be watered down with a quart of water and mixed in a "scuttled butt kept for that purpose and done up on deck, and in the presence of the Lieutenant of the Watch." He also recommended that they add sugar and lime or lemon juice, thereby preventing scurvy among the troops. In short time, the drink became known affectionately by a shortening of his nickname "Old Grosgram" and has been known ever since as "grog."

Rum was on board all British ships and consumed with habitual toasts to the ruler of the period. It was so ubiquitous that legend has it when Admiral Nelson was killed at the Battle of Trafalgar in 1805, his body was preserved in a cask of rum until it could be returned to Great Britain, giving the beverage yet another naval nickname: Nelson's Blood.

For years, the British Virgin Island firm of Pusser's was one of the many companies that supplied the rum to the British Navy, though the ration was reduced to a quarter cup in the 1850s. The grog drinking that Vernon established endured until July 31, 1970, Black Tot Day, when sailors wore black armbands and the last "Up Spirits" was piped.

Rum Row

Rum drinking, whether on a planter's veranda or the deck of a pirate vessel, quickly became a New World passion. Rum became the New World's version of the Old World's demon gin, and soon the poor and indigent—not to mention the enslaved—were besotting themselves at alarming rates. Beginning in the eighteenth century and continuing with greater zeal throughout the nineteenth, concerned United States citizens began to campaign for the regulation of drinking habits and, in many cases, they lobbied for laws regulating the consumption of alcohol. The result was that tavern keepers became creative about the ways in which they sold rum. For example, this was the period of the Striped Pig scam. Patrons would pay a sum to see a "striped pig" (an animal gaudily painted with garish stripes), and while viewing the pig, they would be given a free glass of rum, thereby circumventing all of the newly established temperance rules.

Several years ago, in an old family Bible, I found a copy of the Temperance Pledge that my grandmother had assiduously signed. She would undoubtedly not be happy with my rum-drinking proclivities. She was more than likely thrilled, though, on January 16, 1920, when the signing of the Eighteenth Amendment signaled the start of Prohibition and a tradition older than the country itself was called into question. The Volstead Act, as the amendment was known, was ratified by all but two of the then forty-eight states; Connecticut and Rhode Island declined. For the first time since the colonies became the United States, liquor was verboten and Americans involved in the production, transfer, or sale of any alcoholic beverage were jailed and their property confiscated. Even grape juice was labeled with the warning "will ferment and turn into wine"!

No sooner than the ink was dry on the document than folks began to think of ways to thwart the law. Five miles off the New Jersey coast, a strip of the Atlantic dubbed Rum Row marked the spot where rum runners offloaded their barrels of booze from the Bahamas and the U.S. Virgin Islands. The liquors' value doubled in the transfer and again doubled once it arrived on the mainland and was watered down for customers in speakeasies and other illicit spots.

Rum running provided the wealth of more than one of Nassau's elite Bay Street Boys and lined the pockets of illustrious men like Joseph Kennedy and the criminal Al Capone. While rum was difficult to find in the speakeasies and gin joints of the United States, only a short trip away on the islands of the Caribbean, rum was not only legal, but abundant and consumed with glorious abandon beneath warm skies with hospitable people. This parched period in the history of the United States directly led to the growth of tourism in the Caribbean. Cuba—most specifically Havana—became a tourist mecca as liquor disappeared from the American mainland and thirsty folks boarded ships and even hazarded trips on the newly established seaplanes and flying boats. Pan-American Airways, which was established in 1927, brought hundreds on the one-hour flights from Florida's dry south coast to the daiquiri- and mojito-lubricated hotels and bars of Havana. They celebrated with the slogan, "Fly to Cuba and bathe in Bacardi." The cocktail culture that had begun in the United States in the late nineteenth century soon spread to the Caribbean, where Prohibition brought the well heeled from the cold and dry North to revel in the tropical warmth and flowing rum of the islands.

Bacardi grew into its international reputation during this period. Facundo Bacardi y Maso

arrived in Santiago de Cuba from Spain in 1836 and established himself as a merchant. He entered into partnership in a distillery in 1862 and slowly began to work at transforming the rum of the time. Prior to Bacardi, rum had been an oily and heavy beverage; Bacardi's genius was that he patiently and painstakingly worked out a method that filtered the oiliness out of the rum and created a smooth beverage that could be consumed with all manner of mixers. Bacardi was also a master of marketing. He took a disadvantage—a distillery (or a nearby palm tree, depending on the story) that was bat-infested and transformed it into

a successful business, in the process creating one of the best-known logos in the world: the Bacardi bat.

Although Señor Facundo was gone by the advent of Prohibition, his heirs cornered the Cuban market with their milder and smoother rum and established the Bacardi brand firmly in the American mind as the rum of the tropical cocktail. Its trademark rum—light, crisp, eminently mixable, and always consistent—has become the world's standard.

When Prohibition finally ended in 1933, rum again stocked bar shelves in the United States, but the rum that graced the shelves

How I am missing you

GREETINGS FROM CUBA · ISLE OF BACARDI

RUM 80 PROOF

of the newly opened watering holes had changed—it was lighter, smoother, and went down more easily.

Tourism's Triumphs

The curiosity about the Caribbean region that began with the first wave of Americans heading to Cuba during Prohibition continued. Tourists trickled through the newly built airports in the islands, where local merchants welcomed the visitors with their signature rums. Steel-band music played tinkling notes in Trinidad. In Haiti, rumba-shirted men greeted travelers with a version of "Choucounne"—the Haitian folk song that has become well known to all Caribbean visitors as "Yellowbird." Others were charmed by the Andrews Sisters singing "Rum and Coca-Cola," which was a first hint of the calypso craze to come. A mid-century generation saw Sky Madison savor Havana's romantic potential as he whisked away the Salvation Army girl in *Guys and Dolls*, a Broadway musical that celebrated the city's mystique. So, the Caribbean region retained its association with rum and romance. Americans bellied up to the bars at Sloppy Joe's and El Floridita and were partying at the Havana Hilton when Castro and his men came out of the Sierra Maestre in 1959.

On less volatile islands, the Caribe Hilton—the chain's first venture in the region—was built on a prime strip in Puerto Rico on the outskirts of downtown San Juan. Its bar well stocked with Bacardi, the Hilton's arrival on the scene signaled that the region was open for tourist business. In Haiti, tourists savored Rhum Barbancourt at Oloffson's bar in Port-au-Prince. While gambling at the tables at El Rancho or dancing to the Haitian merengue at the Cabane Choucoune, visitors indulged in all manner of cocktails made with Rhum Barbancourt or one of the flavored rums made by another branch of the family. In Jamaica, British expatriates from Ian Fleming to Noel Coward broke the monotony of gin and tonic with a foray into the world of rum. The Appleton and Myers's companies provided imbibers with a robust mixer, and those who truly wanted to go native could sample Wray and Nephew Overproof rum, the island's 151-proof rum that could allegedly do everything from stretch leather shoes to run a car. The Myrtle Bank Hotel in Kingston was legendary for years for its rum punch, which its bartenders personalized with the addition of a bit of maraschino liqueur, their secret ingredient.

Caribbean singer Harry Belafonte appeared on *The Ed Sullivan Show* on October 11, 1953, on the new medium—television—singing "Matilda" and "Scarlet Ribbons" and some of the tamer calypso ballads by Irving Burgie. Americans of all classes began to think of taking vacations in the lands of yellowbirds and palm trees, where rum flowed like water. Those who couldn't take the trip bought rum at their local liquor stores and re-created the Caribbean at home. Little Japanese umbrellas graced drinks prepared by husbands armed with cocktail shakers and dressed in tropical shirts. People traded recipes for daiquiris while serving frosty Cuba Libres and rum punches poolside in the newly affluent suburban America.

The three-martini lunch and preprandial cocktail dominated the 1960s for the middle class, while the counterculture turned on, tuned in, and dropped out. We all became oenophiles in the 1970s, and then the high-flying 1980s and 1990s relegated the cocktail shakers and cocktail stirrers to the back of the liquor cabinet, if not to the yard sale. The drink of the moment was high-end single-malt Scotch and few indulged in the fun of cocktail mixing in the rush to make more money and display it with premium champagnes and the most expensive, obscure, and elusive brands of alcohol.

Cocktail Culture Returns

Whether the *Sex and the City* crew brought cocktails back or simply brought the urban edginess of cocktail drinking to the larger world, the female foursome contributed greatly to the proliferation of cocktail culture in the twenty-first century, as it once again took over the world. Cosmopolitans became the signature drink of that show, but many consumers passed on the pink drink for the new craze—mojitos. The mint, lime, and rum drink took over the country and brought with it another rum revolution as the liquor once again colonized the hearts and palates of the American public. Restaurants began taking on tropical themes and some of them now even specialize in rum bars, where the clientele are treated to a wide range of rums from a variety of different sources.

Widening patterns of Caribbean migration today are also bringing new Caribbean rums into the American mix as immigrants hold on to the rums of their home countries. Bacardi remains the top-selling rum these days, but patrons increasingly request Rhum Barbancourt or Mount Gay or even Matusalem. Those who sail have learned the virtues of the Bermudan Gosling's Black Seal brand, and those with a reverence for naval traditions may raise a tot of Pusser's. Captain Morgan spiced rum recalls the pirate heritage for the college crowd and it sometimes seems as though new rums are discovered daily as consumers become more informed and more selective. Even French *rhum agricole*, prepared from sugarcane juice instead of molasses, is becoming more available in the United States as its smooth winey taste makes converts of many. The fact that it has its own AOC (*appellation d'origin controlée*) may be a harbinger of what is to come in the world of rum. But whether in a frosty daiquiri, a creamy piña colada, or simply a jelly jar filled with a favorite variety, the Caribbean's beverage of choice is raised high in salute multiple times daily. After all—it's history in a glass.

CAROUSEL LOUNGE IN HOTEL MONTELEONE

NEW ORLEANS, LA.

RHUM KWANGO

SPIRITUEUX

MAISON
J. DESMET-MAERTENS
MENENSTEENWEG 163
RUMBEKE

TEL 051 20653
R C COURTRAI 13 491
CONT 018-048-
070-097L

when RED HEART RUM goes into your PLANTER'S PUNCH you get that finer, tastier Jamaica rum flavor that comes only in

HENRY WHITE & Cᵒˢ RED HEART JAMAICA RUM
LONDON TRADE MARK ENG.

Fill a tall glass with cracked ice. Add a dash of bitters, juice of half lemon, 1 teaspoon sugar, 1½ oz. RED HEART RUM. Shake until cold. Garnish with half slice orange and a cherry.

Famous Since 1842

90 PROOF • NATIONAL DISTILLERS PRODUCTS CORP., NEW YORK, N. Y.

chapter 2

Measurements
and Mixology

A worker is only as good as his tools.

Fortunately, a Caribbean bar is not difficult to set up. Remember that in the islands, *minimal* is the word, so there is no real need for fancy equipment, but some *basic* essentials can help make your drinks as amazing as possible. You need a basic bartender's set of tools and should consider a good blender with a strong motor. Fancy gadgets are far from necessary for a good Caribbean cocktail. Here are some of the necessities plus a few embellishments.

BAR TOWELS: They can be plain white tea towels or have all manner of sayings on them, but the fact remains that there will be spills to clean and glasses that need polishing.

CAN AND BOTTLE OPENERS: Be sure that you have an old-fashioned church key as well as the kind of wine-bottle opener that's often called a waiter's friend. It comes complete with a corkscrew, small knife, and bottle opener on one tool. Have good solid ones and make sure that they're handy.

COCKTAIL SHAKER: An old-fashioned Boston shaker is made of two tumblers that fit tightly together. One tumbler is metal and the other is glass. Shaking the drink allows you to aerate it and create a bit of froth, but most important, it allows you to mix the ingredients thoroughly.

Limit your displays of virtuosity to a few judicious maracas-like shakes in time to the music that's playing.

ELECTRIC BLENDER: An electric blender with a strong motor is a must for a Caribbean bar if you're a lover of frozen daiquiris and piña coladas.

JIGGER: This is the basic measure used for drinks. Usually a two-ended cup, the larger cone holds between 1½ and 2 ounces. The smaller cone is called a "pony" and holds either ¾ or 1 ounce. Whoops—no jigger? Remember that you probably have measuring spoons in your kitchen. Two tablespoons are equal to 1 ounce.

JUICER: You will be amazed at the flavor that real fruit can bring to a drink. You can use an old-fashioned carnival glass juicer like the one that your grandmother probably had. A wooden citrus reamer or the metal juicers that can be found in Latin American markets also work well. All drinks in this book call for fresh juice unless otherwise stated. With most of these you will need to strain the juice. Any small strainer will do for this task.

LONG-HANDLED BAR SPOON: Some drinks do not need shaking, as that will sometimes cloud the final cocktail. These should be stirred gently with a long spoon that is designed to incorporate all of the ingredients.

MUDDLER: Essentially a pestle without the mortar, a muddler allows the bartender to extract the oils from citrus pieces, or mash fruit like strawberries and passion fruit in a glass.

NUTMEG GRATER: Rum punches and other classic Caribbean cocktails need the final fillip of a dash of nutmeg. The stuff that comes out of the can or bottle will simply not do. Get yourself a modest nutmeg grater and top each drink off with a grinding of the real thing.

PARING KNIFE AND CUTTING BOARD: You'll need these in order to cut ingredients down to size for muddling or as garnishes.

STRAINER: More accurately called a *Hawthorne strainer*, this is the familiar round strainer, with a springlike coil around the edge, through which a shaken drink is poured. It is designed to fit snugly over the mouth of the glass section of a cocktail shaker.

SWIZZLE STICK: If you're traveling in the Caribbean, you may be able to find a traditional wooden swizzle stick, which has many spokes radiating from a central stem. If not, simply use a small bar whisk for the same results.

ZESTER: This is a small knife that allows you to separate the zest from the pith of citrus fruit. Some zesters make small zest, while others create larger twists.

Rums and Mixers

Rum comes in many different styles and a well-stocked Caribbean bar will have varieties of each. There are basically two different types: Rum made from molasses and rum made from sugarcane juice.

Molasses-based rums are more common and come from Jamaica, Barbados, Puerto Rico, Cuba, the Dominican Republic, Bermuda, and most of the rest of the Caribbean. This is the style that we are most familiar with. Individual islands and even individual distillers have their own styles; indeed, most distilleries have two or three different types of rum in their repertoires. Increasingly, distillers are aging their rums for a final product that is more complex (and more expensive). Bacardi is known for its perfection as a mixer and many of the rums from the Spanish-speaking areas like Cuba and the Dominican Republic mirror its adaptability. Appleton and Myers's from Jamaica are heartier and valued for their caramel undertones. Gosling's from Bermuda seems dark in the glass, but is light to the taste. Barbados' Mount Gay offers a range of rums from the light silver to the snifter-worthy sugarcane brandy.

Under the umbrella of molasses-based rums, the British style is hearty in Jamaica and smooth in Barbados. The Spanish style in Puerto Rico and the Dominican Republic is made for mixing—think Bacardi in all of its variations. Some of the rums of the Spanish Caribbean and Latin America are remarkably smooth, and there are some prize-winners there, so it's hard to generalize.

The French style has an entirely different taste, as rum in the French-speaking islands is based on sugarcane juice rather than molasses. This gives the rum (they are actually called *rhum*, as I will refer to them in recipes) a winey nose. Many of these rhums are aged in oak for considerable time and take on the taste and depth of a fine old cognac. If you are lucky enough to taste one of these, don't mix it with anything, simply pour it into a snifter and take your time.

Although they have precedent in history, today's spiced rums are geared for a younger American market.

Flavoring Ingredients

These can be used to create your own infused rums or simply as flavoring agents for your Caribbean cocktails.

ALLSPICE: This berry, the size of a large peppercorn, has the taste of nutmeg, cinnamon, black pepper, and cloves. The berries are also known as *Jamaica pepper* and, to the eternal confusion of many, as *pimento*. Infuse it in rum and you've got a variation of Pimento Dram (page 104), a classic Jamaican liqueur.

Allspice is readily available in supermarkets. Purchase whole berries, not the powdered form. Also note that the berries can vary widely in size so use your own judgment when a recipe calls for a certain number.

CANE SYRUP: This light-colored sugar syrup has a hint of the molasses taste of sugarcane. It's used in preparing the 'ti punch and punch vieux that are the ubiquitous drinks of the French Antilles. A simple sugar syrup (page 39) is a good substitute.

Another version of cane syrup is that from Louisiana, which goes by the name of *melao de cana* in the Spanish-speaking world or *sirop de batterie* in the French one. This heavy, dark syrup is made from pressed sugarcane but is lighter in taste than molasses. Steen's, the brand of choice in Louisiana, can be ordered via mail (see page 162). If you're fortunate enough to make it to the farmers' market in New Orleans, you may purchase cane syrup prepared from heirloom canes by local farmers.

CINNAMON: The rolled-up quill of the dried pale-brown inner bark of the cinnamon tree was one of the most precious spices of the ancient Romans. Known generically as "spice" to people in the English-speaking Caribbean, it grows in the Caribbean, where it is commonly used along with its coarser, close cousin, cassia. When purchasing it, look for the quills and not the ground spice. You can grind your own in a spice or coffee grinder that is kept for this purpose. You should look for quills that are highly aromatic and keep them in an airtight container so that they do not lose their potency. Long quills make an interesting garnish to some hot drinks that use the spice as an ingredient.

CURACAO: This is an orange-flavored liqueur named for one of the islands of the Netherlands Antilles on which it is produced. It is readily available in liquor stores. Blue curaçao often turns up in Caribbean cocktails, as its color allows the final mixed drink to have the blue of a tropical lagoon.

FALERNUM: This sugar syrup takes its name from a Roman wine. It is flavored with almond, ginger, cloves, and lime, and may contain hints of vanilla, allspice, or other ingredients. It's used in many tropical beverages in place of simple syrup and may or may not be alcoholic. It's mainly used in the southern Caribbean and most commonly in Barbados, where it is one of the ingredients in Corn and Oil (the other is rum!). You can purchase falernum online (see page 162) or make your own (page 41).

GINGER: This rhizome of a tropical plant is probably a native of Asia. It has done so well in the New World, though, that Jamaican ginger has become well known. Ginger is used fresh, dried, or powdered in many of the region's recipes and it turns up in ginger beers.

If purchasing powdered ginger, look for Jamaican, which is more delicate in flavor. Purchase rhizome ginger when it is firm. It can be refrigerated wrapped in paper towels or plastic bags. Don't forget that ginger ale and the less common ginger beer can add a gingery zing to drinks along with a bit of fizz. A simple syrup prepared from ginger juice (page 39) is another lovely addition to a drink.

GRENADINE: If it's pink and a drink, it's probably got grenadine in it somewhere. This syrup was originally made from pomegranate juice and its name comes from *grenade*, the French word for pomegranate, which also gives its name to the island of Grenada. Today's grenadines are more often than not prepared from artificial ingredients, but now that pomegranate juice has become quite readily available, it's time to attempt to make your own grenadine (page 40).

GUAVABERRY LIQUEUR: Although I had my first taste of guavaberry liqueur in St. Croix, the beverage is the national drink of St. Maarten. Prepared from the fruit of the guavaberry bush—no relation to the guava—the liqueur is a holiday tradition on the Dutch side of the island, where carolers used to go from house to house singing, "Good morning, good morning; I come for me guavaberry" before being treated to a taste of the host's homemade potion. Today, you can purchase guavaberry liqueur when traveling to St. Maarten, online, or occasionally in U.S. liquor stores.

MALIBU: This is a favorite brand of sweet coconut-flavored rum from Barbados. It's a popular mixer and sold in more than eighty countries. It's readily available and good straight or as a mixer. Try some in a piña colada.

MAUBY: I have a postcard from the early 1900s that shows a Caribbean mauby seller from Guadeloupe (facing page, top left). She's seated next to a tray full of bottles, looking at the camera with a bottle in her hand, and dressed in traditional *grande robe* with a headtie around her carefully coiffed hair. Standing over her is a bare-chested workman in torn pants who is drinking thirstily from a bottle of mauby.

Mauby, called *mabi* in French, is a local beverage in much of the Caribbean. Until fairly recently, it was common to see vendors in the main streets of Caribbean towns with

containers of mauby balanced on their heads, and virtually every housewife had her own purveyor.

The traditional beverage is prepared from the fruit and bark of several small fragrant Caribbean trees: *Columbrina elliptica* or *Columbrina aborescens*. The liquid is then diluted with water, flavored with vanilla, and sweetened with sugar. There are many different recipes for preparation, but several include aniseed. The drink can be fermented as a sort of root beer with a kick or consumed unfermented. Mauby is reputed to have a variety of medicinal uses, ranging from curing children's ailments to calming stomachaches. It's a sort of root beer panacea. Today, things have changed; mauby is not simply sold in markets as bits of bark and twigs, but it is packaged in cellophane and even sold in bottled form to be diluted to taste. Since the method of preparation will depend on the type of mauby you find, I will leave this one up to you. Simply follow the package directions. Then add ice and savor.

MOLASSES: Called *melasse* in French and *melao de cana* in Spanish, this by-product of sugarcane refining is a spicy thread that runs through the history of blacks in the New World. Molasses was one of the Americas' principal sweeteners until the middle of the nineteenth century. It is easily available at the supermarket near the sugar products. Try using a spoonful instead of sugar in lemonade or limeade.

NUTMEG AND MACE: Two of the spices that Columbus was looking for when he stumbled upon the Caribbean—nutmeg and mace—are from the same tree. The nutmeg is the seed and the mace is the lacy aril that covers it. Grenada, the Caribbean's Spice Island, is one of the world's largest producers of nutmeg today. Nutmeg has been a popular spice in Caribbean cocktails for centuries and a grating is indispensable to a true rum punch.

Get a nutmeg grater and whole nuts, which will release a small bit of oil when pressed if they are good quality. Buy in small quantities and store in an airtight container, as nutmeg rapidly loses its aroma. (Nutmeg novices should know that the nutmeg may come within its shell. The red casing on the outside is mace; remove it, then crack the shell to get at the nutmeg.)

ORGEAT: This almond-flavored syrup is a mix of almonds and orange flower water and may contain barley water. It can be used solo or mixed with water. In the Spanish-speaking world, it is the basis of the summer drink *horchata*, but it is also used as an ingredient in several mixed drinks, such as mai tais. Orgeat can be found in specialty stores and Spanish markets or ordered online (see page 162).

SORREL: The deep red flower of the hibiscus family is sometimes known as roselle (rosella) and in Spanish as *flor de Jamaica*. It is African in origin and is consumed in Egypt under the name of *carcade* or *karkade*. The podlike flowers of the plant are dried and steeped in water to make a brilliant red drink that has a slightly tart taste. It is a traditional Christmas drink with or without rum. Formerly found in Caribbean markets at Christmastime, sorrel is now available in them almost year-round. Fresh sorrel is available at Christmastime.

SUGARCANE: This "honey-bearing reed" was brought to the Caribbean from the Canary Islands by Columbus on his second voyage in 1493. Until recently, the refined superfine white sugar crystals have been most popular. Many people now prefer the pure cane taste of Muscovado (a.k.a. Barbados) or Demerara sugar, which is the last sugar in the barrel after the molasses has been drained off. Sugarcane can be mail-ordered or occasionally found in Caribbean and Asian neighborhoods. The sweet juice known as *gurapo* in Cuba is an interesting base on which to build a cocktail. Long, thin sticks cut from sugarcane stalks can be used as garnishes in drinks or as skewers for cocktail nibbles.

TIA MARIA: A Jamaican coffee liqueur, Tia Maria was invented in Jamaica around World War I. It is a mix of Jamaican Blue Mountain coffee and other ingredients. It's a prime mixer for making a Jamaican coffee with good Jamaican rum.

VANILLA: The pods of this relative of an orchid develop their deep coloring and taste after a

STACKING BAGS OF RAW SUGAR

lengthy period of processing. First used by the Aztecs, vanilla is one of the world's master spices and is used in much of the baking of the Creole world. Anyone who has seen the fat, oily beans in the market in Guadeloupe will opt to prepare their own extract by adding a vanilla bean to a small vial of dark rum for a particularly Caribbean addition. Make your own vanilla rum by infusing a few vanilla beans in the alcohol. Just pop them in, replace the top, and let the bottle sit in a cool place for a week or so. Voila!

The Bitter and the Sweet

Drinks are often enhanced by a dash or two of something other than the alcohols that go into their mixing. Often these add a subtle bitterness or give the drink the hint of sweetness that makes it sing. The complexity that is given by these additions is one of the things that distinguishes a professionally made potion from that of a mere amateur.

BITTERS: Bitters are alcohols that have been infused with the essence of herbs and roots. Essentially they're tinctures and they are often as strong as 80 or 90 proof. They were originally marketed in Europe as digestive aids. Bitters certainly are known for settling upset stomachs and a dash or two in a glass of club soda or ginger ale can work wonders for the queasy. Even though they're used in small quantities, bitters should not be used in nonalcoholic beverages because they contain alcohol and could be harmful to those who are allergic to it. For those without such allergies, a dash of

bitters in a French lemonade gives the fizz complexity and makes it seem more adult. Popular bitters include such brands as Angostura, which are the classic Caribbean brand, and Peychaud's, which are from New Orleans.

There is a second category of bitters that includes beverages such as Campari or Fernet Branca or Cynar. They, too, have their digestive claims, and a small glass of Fernet Branca or a dash or two in a glass of water or soda is considered a hangover cure by some hard-drinking folks I know. These bitters can be consumed as aperitifs, but a dash or two can also be used to add complexity to cocktails.

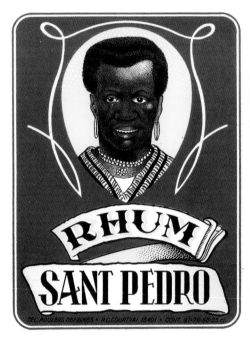

Some folks are making their own bitters today and myriad recipes can be found on the Web. Jamie Boudreau has an interesting post including a do-it-yourself recipe for cherry bitters on SpiritsandCocktails .com. Those with less initiative may want to just go to the Fee Brothers Web site (see page 162). It's a bartender's secret source and offers six types of bitters including orange bitters, mint bitters, peach bitters, and grapefruit bitters. You can order Peychaud's through the Sazerac company Web site (see page 162).

SWEETS: Simple syrup is just what it claims to be: a syrup that is simple to prepare. It is a sweetening agent and is used in most drinks to counterpoint the acidity of lemon or lime. It can also be used to sweeten everything from iced tea to mixed drinks. There are numerous ways to prepare simple syrup; the easiest and most common is to use one part water to one part sugar. Others prefer a heavier syrup and use two parts sugar to one water.

Simple Syrup

I'm a two-to-one person. You can just use one cup of sugar if you prefer.

makes about 1 cup

2 cups sugar
1 cup water

Combine the sugar and water in a small saucepan and bring to a simmer over medium heat, stirring occasionally. Continue to simmer and stir until all of the sugar has dissolved, about 3 minutes. Allow the syrup to cool to room temperature and then pour it into a sterilized decorative bottle that can be fitted with a speed pourer. The syrup will keep in the refrigerator for 1 month.

Ginger Syrup

You can prepare a ginger syrup by substituting ginger juice for half of the liquid in the simple syrup recipe. Make ginger juice by grating ginger into cheesecloth and squeezing it, or purchase it from www.gingerpeople.com.

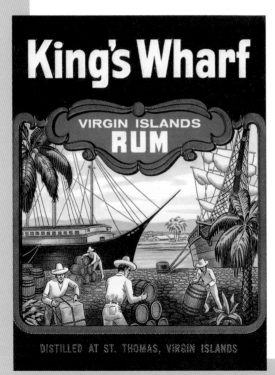

Grenadine

You can prepare grenadine by replacing the water in the simple syrup recipe with pomegranate juice, which is readily available.

Lavender Syrup

Once you've mastered the simple syrup, then it's a short step to making your own flavor-infused syrups. Try a simple lavender syrup. It can be used to sweeten lemonade and as a cooling drink with the addition of club soda or plain tap water.

makes about 2½ cups

3 cups water
½ cup lavender flowers
3 cups sugar

Put the water and lavender flowers in a 3-quart saucepan and bring to a boil over medium heat. Lower the heat and allow it to simmer for 3 to 5 minutes. Remove from the heat and allow it to infuse for 5 minutes.

Strain the liquid into a bowl, pressing down on the lavender flowers to make sure that all of the liquid is released. Return the liquid to the saucepan and add the sugar. Stir until all of the sugar is dissolved and then bring to a simmer over medium heat. Remove the syrup from the heat and allow it to cool. Decant it into a sterilized bottle. (I use the stoppered bottles that French lemonade comes in and boil them and remove the labels before use.)

The syrup will keep in the refrigerator for several weeks.

Mint Syrup

Prepare as for lavender syrup, substituting 3 tablespoons minced fresh peppermint leaves and 2 tablespoons minced fresh spearmint leaves for the lavender. This liquid is a perfect way to keep the minty flavor at its peak in a mojito.

Hot and Sweet Syrup

makes about ¾ cup

1 cup water
3 ounces fresh ginger, smashed
½ teaspoon black peppercorns, crushed
¼ teaspoon minced jalapeño chile
1 cup sugar

Put the water, ginger, peppercorns, and chile in a small nonreactive saucepan and bring to a boil over medium heat. Lower the heat and allow it to simmer for 3 to 5 minutes. Remove from the heat and allow it to infuse for 5 minutes.

Strain the liquid into a bowl, pressing down on the solids to make sure that all of the liquid is released. Return the liquid to the saucepan and add the sugar. Stir until all of the sugar is dissolved and then bring to a simmer over medium heat. Remove the syrup from the heat and allow it to cool. It will keep in the refrigerator for several weeks.

Planting Sugar Cane.

Falernum

Falernum is a sweetening agent that is used in Barbados and that is difficult to find Stateside. Adjust the flavorings to suit your taste. I like mine a little sweet.

makes 1 liter

12 limes, zested
2 tablespoons sugar
8 whole cloves
Dash of almond extract
1 liter Barbadian-style white rum, such as
    Mount Gay or Cockspur

Put the zest, sugar, cloves, and almond extract in a large glass container or jar, add the rum, and loosely cover. Keep in a sunny place for 4 days. Strain it to remove the solids and pour the liquid into a bottle that can be fitted with a speed pourer. The falernum will keep for several months at room temperature.

Caribbean Spiced Sugar

Some cocktails look especially pretty when presented in a sugar-rimmed glass. Prepare your own mixture of sugar that combines all of the flavors of the island of Grenada, the region's very own spice island.

makes 1½ cups

½ cup dark brown Muscovado sugar
1 cup superfine sugar
2 teaspoons ground cinnamon
1 teaspoon ground nutmeg
½ teaspoon ground mace
¼ teaspoon ground allspice

Put the sugar in the bowl of a heavy mortar or a food processor and pound or grind it until it is reduced to fine crystals. Then add the remaining ingredients to the bowl and stir to mix until well combined. This will keep for several weeks in a glass jar. When ready to use, pour it into a saucer and lightly wet the rim of the glass. Dip it in the sugar and you're ready to go.

III. Un tout petit verre !
P.C.P.

A SUGAR CANE MILL

Island Style

GLASSES: The French have a saying: "The eyes eat first." I could adapt it to Caribbean cocktails and say, "The eyes drink first." An attractive, appetizing cocktail is what you want, so glasses are important. Before you've made a drink, ask yourself what kind of glass will best show this off? Or, what type of glass will give your drink a bit of extra flair? There is such an abundance of choice today that the mind boggles.

Glass types that are given with the recipes are only suggestions, not hard and fast rules. If you prefer a stemmed glass as I do, use it even if you're drinking a tall colada. Your glasses are an extension of your own taste and, just as you would personalize the drink they contain, you should personalize the glasses. A final note: remember, glasses do not have to be purchased in sets. What better way to distinguish an individual's drink than by having each drink in a different glass? Think of all of those different heirloom glasses and those unmatched ones that lurk at the back of the closet. Now's the time to get them out, wash them to a bright sparkle, and use them. That's one way not to lose your drink at a cocktail party.

The basic glass types follow, but don't be afraid to be adventurous. If you like a stemmed glass—use it. Love that jelly jar with the decorations of red flowers that you remember from childhood? Use it! This is the time to have fun.

Bucket Glass (Old Fashioned): Short and squat with a thick base, this type of glass will come in handy when you make a caipirinha or any drink that requires a muddler. Sizes range from 6 to 8 ounces and it's usually used for simple drinks like rum and soda.

Champagne Flute: Years ago Champagne was served in saucers allegedly shaped like Marie Antoinette's breast. The long, thin flutes came into favor around the 1980s and are great because the bubbles keep longer. The smaller 6-ounce flutes are good for sours and the larger 10-ounce flutes can serve for other light cocktails that require a bit of flair.

Collins (Highball): This tall, thin, 8- to 10-ounce glass can be used for any drink that needs a bit of ice or that needs soda to top it off. It can be perfect for a dark and stormy or a rum punch.

Fruit Containers: Don't forget that pineapples can be hollowed out and make perfect drink containers, as do brown coconuts. I've even seen small melons used.

Hurricane (Poco Grande): This curvaceous glass is named for the rum drink that is the hallmark of Pat O'Brien's in New Orleans. It's a classic Caribbean bar glass used for everything from piña coladas to shandys.

Irish Coffee Glass: This heat-resistant glass usually resembles a footed mug and is used for hot beverages like grogs.

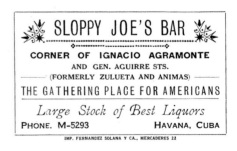

7002. Cutting Sugar Cane, Cuba.

National Hotel. Havana Cuba

measurements and mixology

Julep Cup: This classic silver cup conjures up images of the Kentucky Derby and drinks sipped on white columned verandas. In the Caribbean, though, the silver mug is put to good use serving rum juleps.

Martini: The triangular shape of a martini glass evokes thoughts of cool frosty gin with a whiff of vermouth. Think of it, though, when you need a glass that can be quickly chilled and will keep a drink cool since the fingers never touch the bowl. This makes it perfect for a classic daiquiri.

Pilsner: This is the typical 10- to 14-ounce tapered, footed beer glass that can work as an all-purpose glass when serving a tall drink that requires ice.

Snifter: This glass has a low foot, wide bowl, and a tapered mouth, and was created for savoring the finest brandies and cognacs. It's designed to warm the liquid in the hands and concentrate its aroma. Some aged rums from the French Caribbean and some top-label brands from the rest of the region demand the respect of a snifter.

GARNISHES: Now that you have the perfect glass, it's time to consider the small elements that will make the finished drink look professional. Sure, there are swizzle sticks and flexible straws and plastic floating mermaids that can hook over the edge of the glass. The following garnishes, though, are natural and will add a bit of Caribbean flair and flavor to your concoctions and make you look like a major mixologist.

Sugarcane: This is the raw material for the beverages in this book, but if you can obtain a stalk of it, cut it down into stirring spears with a very sharp knife. (Be extremely careful with cutting it, as it is hard to do! See page 138 for directions.)

Citrus Fruit: Certainly limes can be sliced and placed on the edge of a glass, but how boring. Think instead of curls of zest cascading from the side of a glass or a pinwheel of mixed citrus fruit skewered with a long toothpick or a *banderilla* of wedges of blood orange, lime, and grapefruit (you can add lemon, too). Use the color of the fruit and the flexibility of the peel (remember to remove as much of the white pith as possible), and your only limit is your imagination.

Coconut: Toast curls of fresh coconut meat that has been shaved with a vegetable peeler for great cocktail nibbles (page 130). They're also perfect when crumbled on top of piña coladas and other coconut-flavored drinks.

Cucumber: Spears of cucumber are not just for Pimm's cups. They are also good in savory drinks like Bloody Marys or in cooling drinks like an Isle of Pines.

Flowers: Mother Nature's own decorations can be used to enhance any Caribbean cocktail; just be sure to consult a botanist or the local botanical garden or check online to make sure they're edible before you end up with a party disaster. Look for edible flowers in the produce section of your grocery.

Herbs: No one would attempt a mojito without spearmint, so think of adding herbs as garnish. Why not garnish a high-octane lime-ade with a sprig of peppermint or add a little *je ne sais quoi* to a Bloody Mary with a bit of cilantro? Decide which fresh herb will set off the flavors of your drink to your liking, then proceed judiciously.

Husk Tomatoes: Also called *tomatillos*, these small sweet tomatoes have a papery outer skin that can be pulled back to display them. Add a tall wooden skewer and voilà—a beautiful drink! Small cherry tomatoes can do the same job, but they're not nearly as exotic or exciting.

Kiwi: When slightly underripe, kiwis can be peeled and cut into circles that can be slit on one side to fit over any glass. They give a welcome change from the citrus that usually is presented there.

Melon: Getting serious about garnishing? Then, it's time to invest in a melon baller. Try a skewer of watermelon, cantaloupe, and honeydew balls or a single melon ball instead of a maraschino cherry. They add color and flavor to any tall drink.

Okra: I've never let an opportunity go by to use okra in some form. A pod of pickled okra is a perfect way to finish off a rum Bloody Mary. Use hot okra for additional zing to the drink.

Olives: These are a no-brainer and perfect in any savory drink. Don't forget the wide array of olives currently available. I'm a sucker for the ones that are stuffed with anchovies, but you may prefer the almond- or blue cheese–stuffed olives.

Pineapple: There's nothing that quite does the job as well as a spear of sweet, slightly acidic pineapple. Try the sweetest one you can find in your next piña colada and you'll understand why it's such a classic.

Spices: Two spices are traditionally used as garnishes in the region. Cinnamon sticks are used in drinks both cold and hot. Look for extra-long quills (some of the longest I've ever seen I purchased in the Plaza del Mercado in San Juan, Puerto Rico). And as for nutmeg, it simply wouldn't be a rum punch without a grinding of fresh nutmeg on the top. Get yourself a nutmeg grater and use it fresh each and every time.

Strawberries: They do grow in the Caribbean region. I remember decades ago watching in amazement as women brought them down from the hills above Port au Prince, Haiti. Use them sparingly; one or two should do the trick as a garnish for strawberry daiquiris.

Umbrellas: It wouldn't be a Caribbean cocktail without a fancy Japanese umbrella somewhere. Check the Internet sources (see page 162) and you can get some of your very own to play with.

A Colorful Cornucopia of Caribbean Fruit

Caribbean drinks gain their brilliant color and fantastic taste from the use of the region's bounty of tropical fruit. Here are some that might turn up in your glass.

BANANAS: Any northerner who journeys to the Caribbean is astonished at the number of varieties of bananas. They range in size from the tiny, delicate ones with slightly sharp taste known as *bananes-figues* in the French-speaking Caribbean to large black-skinned ripe ones. Because of their form, they have always been identified with sexuality. In French Creole the small ones are called "go get dressed little boy" and the large ones, "Oh, Mama. God help me!"

Bananas are major players in several Caribbean cocktails for their creaminess and taste. Bananas should be purchased when their skins are unblemished and they are firm to the touch. They should never be refrigerated or they'll begin to turn black.

CARAMBOLA: Called *star fruit* or *five-fingered fruit*, this multisided fruit becomes a translucent yellow when ripe. Its juice is consumed in the Caribbean and it is frequently used as a garnish in drinks. If you wish to juice them, the pale, slightly acidic juice adds a wonderful fillip to fruit punches and is great on its own with rum. Carambola is readily available at specialty greengrocers.

CHERIMOYA: Sometimes called the *custard apple*, this fist-sized fruit has a custard-like flesh that tastes like a mixture of vanilla ice cream and banana. Cherimoyas range in color from green to grayish brown to black. They are frequently used as the basis for fabulous beverages. A cherimoya should be eaten when it gives slightly when pressed with a finger and has a characteristically sweetish smell. They are found fresh only in specialty shops and in the subtropical areas of the United States. The rest of us have to content ourselves with canned or frozen pulp and juice.

CHILES: These fruits cross-pollinate with the alacrity of rabbits and have different names wherever you find them. There are Scotch Bonnet, wiri wiri, bird peppers, and more in the Caribbean, where the milder ones turn up occasionally as garnishes in drinks.

COCONUT: No one is exactly sure how the coconut arrived in the New World. They are thought to have originated in Southeast Asia, but the nut floats and it seems to have arrived in this hemisphere before the Europeans. For centuries, the coconut palm was virtually the staff of life for the peoples of the Caribbean.

In the summer in many Caribbean neighborhoods, jelly coconuts (the green fruit whose meat is still a jellylike mass) are hawked on the streets by vendors who open them and then pour the coconut water into plastic containers. And of course there are always the hairy brown coconuts that peer out at us from greengrocers' bins with whimsical faces made from their "eyes." They can be transformed into coconut milk, grated coconut, and just about any other coconut product you may need; they also make great serving vessels for many drinks.

Note that the liquid in a coconut is coconut *water*. Coconut *milk* is what results when grated coconut meat is infused in coconut water. Alternatively, if you're in a real pinch, unsweetened canned coconut milk can be used. Some piña colada recipes call for cream of coconut, a canned thicker liquid. Coco Lopez is the brand to get.

SAINT-PIERRE DE LA MARTINIQUE — USINE DE RHUM ET DE SUCRE

To prepare coconut milk, open a brown or dry coconut by heating it in a medium oven for 10 minutes. (The coconut will develop "fault" lines.) Remove from the oven and use a hammer to break open the coconut along the "fault" lines. Remove the shell, scrape off the brown peel, and grate the white coconut meat. (You should get 1½ to 2 cups of tightly packed grated coconut. Using a food processor prevents skinned fingers.) Add 1 cup of heated coconut water or 1 cup boiling water to the grated coconut meat and allow the mixture to stand for half an hour. Strain the mixture though cheesecloth, squeezing the pulp to get all of the coconut milk.

GUAVA: This fruit is native to the Americas; there are over 100 edible varieties. A rich source of minerals and vitamins A and C, guavas are eaten at various stages of their development. When green, they are slightly tart; when ripe, they are sweeter. In the Caribbean, guava juice is popular and often found prepackaged in supermarkets. Try Loosa or Ceres brands or one of the Israeli varieties that will give your drinks the true flavor of this tropical fruit.

KIWI: Originally from China, this green fruit used to be known as the Chinese gooseberry until the 1950s. Its name change and marketing history are the stuff of business school textbooks and now the fuzzy-skinned green fruit that tastes of bananas and strawberries is virtually ubiquitous. Kiwis turn up as garnishes in the Caribbean and they can also be juiced, but strain out the seeds if juicing, as they will make the liquid bitter.

LIMES: Caribbean limes are similar to Key limes with thin greenish-yellow skins that turn yellow when overripe. Limes are the prime ingredient in most of the region's drinks. In the French-speaking islands of the region, they are cut *en palettes*: sliced around the outside of the fruit's center core so that each wedge is seedless. They are served at the side of the plate as condiments along with rum and sugar for the preparation of the French Caribbean's ubiquitous 'ti punch. Caribbean limes rarely make their way to northern markets. Instead, select the juiciest regular (Persian) limes that you can find with no blemishes or soft spots, or purchase Key limes.

MANGO: This tropical fruit par excellence is known by some as "the king of the fruits." More than 326 varieties have been recorded in India, although the fruit is thought to have originated in the Malaysian archipelago. Mangoes arrived in the New World (Brazil) in the fifteenth century and in the Caribbean after 1872. The most common mangoes in the Caribbean are Julie mangoes, which are flattened, light green ovals.

Mangoes are often pureed in drinks. Sucking the juice out of a ripe mango is one of the messier liquid delights of the region. Once a hard-to-find specialty fruit, mangoes are becoming more readily available in the States and Europe. If you cannot find them at regular greengrocers, look in shops selling Caribbean and tropical produce. Mangoes should be purchased when they are firm but yield slightly to the touch. A sniff will tell you if they are aromatic and ripe.

ORANGE: Oranges are so common that we give them culinary short shrift, but a fresh squirt of orange juice can brighten up any cocktail. Bitter oranges are the basis of the Caribbean liqueur known as curaçao and blood oranges are making their way into the drinks lexicon of the region. Oranges, like all citrus, should be selected when they are heavy for their size, as this indicates that they are juicy. As with all citrus, bottled juice is no substitute and canned is unthinkable!

PASSION FRUIT: The fruit from the passion-flower can resemble a thick-skinned yellow or purple plum. Inside, numerous small black seeds are encased in a yellow- or orange-colored translucent flesh, which is wonderfully tart and almost citrusy. Called *maracudja* in some parts of the French-speaking Caribbean and *granadille* in others, it's called *granadilla* in the Spanish-speaking Caribbean (where the juice is known as *parcha*).

Better known for its juice, passion fruit's tart taste can be found in drinks throughout the region. The juice's distinctive flavor can be found in numerous liqueurs mixed with everything from rum to cognac, and many commercial fruit juice mixes. Fresh passion fruit is increasingly available in the northern United States and the juice and passion fruit–flavored liqueurs (such as Alizé) are readily available.

PINEAPPLE: While many of us connect pineapples with Hawaii, they were first seen by Europeans in the Caribbean. Columbus noted them on his journey to Guadeloupe in 1493. Although they're familiar to Americans, most of us have not savored the rich sweet taste of a pineapple that has ripened to maturity in the sun. The flavor when combined with that of fresh coconut is the hallmark of a perfect Caribbean piña colada (page 82). You can tell a ripe pineapple by its heft (it should feel heavy for its size) and by its aromatic smell. Canned pineapple or canned pineapple juice is no substitute for the juice of the ripe fruit unless you're stranded on an iceberg!

POMELO: *Chadec* is the French name for this thick-skinned fruit, also called a shaddock. Thought to be the ancestor of the grapefruit, the fruit is used for juice; grapefruit can be substituted.

SOURSOP: The shape of this tropical fruit has earned it the nickname of *bullock's heart* in some countries. Inside the spiny, leathery, dark-green skin, the pulp is white and creamy and slightly granular. Called *corossol* in the French-speaking Caribbean and *guanabana* in the Spanish-speaking countries, the soursop is native to the Caribbean and northern South America. It can also have a smooth green or greenish brown skin. Outside of the region, the fruit is usually consumed raw or in juices like Cuba's Champola or Puerto Rico's Carato.

The soursop rarely appears in northern markets, as they don't travel well. However, if you're lucky, select one that is slightly soft to the touch without too many blemishes. The pulp is also available frozen.

TAMARIND: This tropical tree produces a brown pod that is processed into an acidulated pulp used for flavoring. Tamarind can be purchased in shops selling Indian products as well as those selling Caribbean products. It usually comes in the form of a prepared pulp, which can be kept for a week or longer in the refrigerator. Prepared tamarind can also be frozen. Tamarind juice is also available, but use with caution as it can have prodigious laxative qualities.

UGLI: This grapefruit-sized fruit isn't ugly at all. It is a cross between a grapefruit, an orange, and a tangerine—often called tangelo. It is a fruit of Jamaican origin and has a sweet citrus taste. It appears on Caribbean tables as juice and marmalade, and glazed and dipped in chocolate in candies. Ugli fruit can occasionally be found in supermarkets or at the greengrocers.

WATERMELON: An immigrant to the Caribbean, the watermelon is believed to have originated in southern Africa. Its high water content makes it perfect for quenching summer thirsts. The flesh can range in hue from pale orange to bright red. Seeded or seedless, thin skinned or thick, the watermelon means summer to many and is perfect for juicing. On the Caribbean's Mexican coast, watermelon *agua frescas* are refreshers that are sold streetside, while other parts of the region simply use the fruit wedges as garnishes for drinks.

Folks thump and shake and sniff, but there are really few sure ways of picking a sweet watermelon other than tasting it. The juice is a great and unexpected addition to fruit punches and goes surprisingly well with white rum.

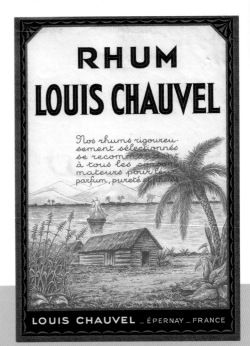

Liquid Measurements

Bar spoon = ½ ounce

1 teaspoon = ⅙ ounce

1 tablespoon = ½ ounce

2 tablespoons (pony) = 1 ounce

3 tablespoons (jigger) = 1½ ounces

¼ cup = 2 ounces

⅓ cup = 3 ounces

½ cup = 4 ounces

⅔ cup = 5 ounces

¾ cup = 6 ounces

1 cup = 8 ounces

1 pint = 16 ounces

1 quart = 32 ounces

750 ml bottle = 25.4 ounces

1 liter bottle = 33.8 ounces

1 medium lemon = 3 tablespoons juice

1 medium lime = 2 tablespoons juice

1 medum orange = ⅓ cup juice

Ingenio de Azucar. Cuba.

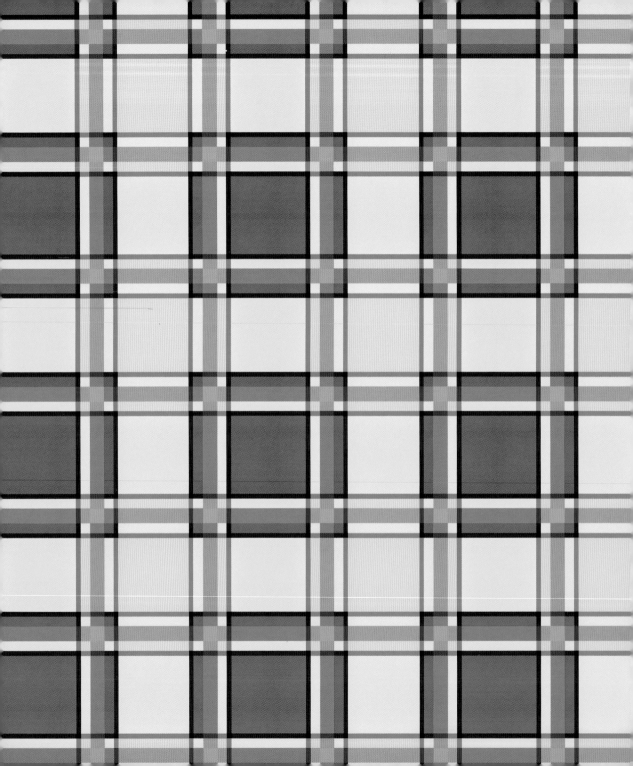

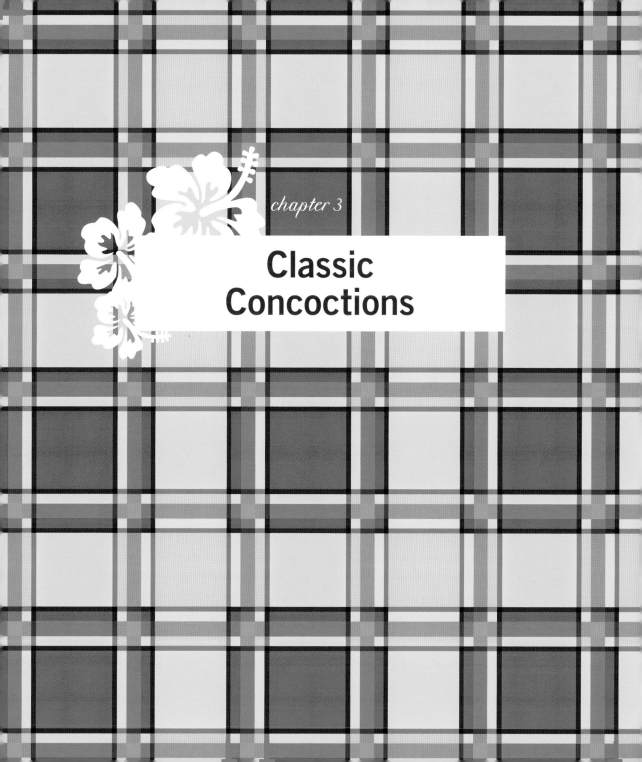

chapter 3

Classic
Concoctions

Rum Punch

makes 1 drink

The first punches were undoubtedly made to mellow some of the harsh taste from rum that had not attained its present smoothness. The name seems to come from the Persian *panj* or the Hindi word *panch*, meaning "five," a reference to the original beverage, which may have been prepared from five ingredients: arrack, sugar, lime juice, spice, and water.

No one is really sure where the first rum punch was made, but the classic Caribbean punch even has its own rhyme to help imbibers remember the correct proportions for preparing it:

One of Sour;
Two of Sweet;
Three of Strong;
Four of Weak;
Serve well-chilled and over ice;
Top with a grinding of nutmeg spice.

1 ounce freshly squeezed strained lime juice

2 ounces Simple Syrup (page 39)

3 ounces Barbadian-style dark rum, such as Mount Gay

4 ounces water

Ice cubes

Freshly grated nutmeg

1 slice citrus for garnish (optional)

Mix the lime juice, simple syrup, rum, and water in a cocktail shaker with ice cubes. Stir well, then pour into a chilled, large highball glass and top with a sprinkling of fresh nutmeg. Garnish with citrus slice, if desired. Serve immediately.

Myrtle Bank Rum Punch

makes 1 drink

The Myrtle Bank Hotel in Jamaica was the place to head in the days when tourists actually went to Kingston. During Prohibition, they would sit on the porch and sip rum punches. The Myrtle Bank Rum Punch is legendary and for years no one knew the secret ingredient. It's maraschino liqueur—an ingredient that turns up in several Caribbean drinks of that period.

2 ounces Jamaican-style dark rum, such as Appleton or Myers's

1 ounce freshly squeezed strained lime juice

1 teaspoon superfine sugar

½ ounce grenadine

Ice cubes

Crushed ice

Club soda

Maraschino liqueur

Combine the rum, lime juice, sugar, and grenadine in a cocktail shaker with ice cubes. Shake vigorously. Strain into a highball glass filled with crushed ice. Top with club soda and float a slick of maraschino liqueur on the top by slowly pouring a teaspoon of the liqueur over the back of a spoon into the glass. Serve immediately.

Planter's Punch

makes 1 drink

Fruit juice–driven Planter's Punch is often an appalling mixture of canned or bottled juices. It moves to another level altogether when it is prepared with fresh juices. For years, Myers's of Jamaica has marketed itself as the Planter's Punch rum.

2 ounces Jamaican-style dark rum, such as Myers's

½ ounce freshly squeezed strained lime juice

2 teaspoons Simple Syrup (page 39)

Dash of grenadine

3 to 4 ice cubes

1 maraschino cherry for garnish

1 slice orange for garnish

Combine the rum, lime juice, simple syrup, and grenadine in a cocktail shaker with the ice cubes. Shake vigorously and taste. Add more simple syrup if needed. Strain into a highball glass. Garnish with the cherry and slice of orange. Serve immediately.

'Ti Punch

This is a classic drink of the Creole world. A bit of sugar, plus a few pieces of limes just off the tree, cut and pressed to express their juice, and enough white rum to give you a buzz. It is, in fact, a French Antillean cousin of Brazil's caipirinha. In some parts of the French-speaking Caribbean, it's known as a C.R.S. for its three ingredients: citron (lime), rhum (no translation necessary!), and sucre (sugar). 'Ti punches are absolutely habit-forming and quite lethal.

1 lime, cut into palettes (see page 47)

1 heaping teaspoon unrefined Muscovado or Demerara sugar (see Notes)

2 ounces white *rhum agricole*, such as Rhum Dillon (see Notes)

Put the lime pieces in an old-fashioned (bucket) glass or a small wide-mouthed stemmed glass. Add the sugar and pour in the rhum. Stir until well mixed. Taste and adjust the sugar and rhum as desired. Serve immediately

NOTES
• I prefer Muscovado or Demerara sugar in these because you get the molasses hit of the sugar and the cane taste of the rhum.

• You may use any white rum, but the white *rhum agricole* of the French Caribbean has a sugarcane-y flavor that is not duplicated in the white rums from the rest of the region.

Martyred on the Grill

If it's August, I know it's time to make my annual trek from Martha's Vineyard down to the Caribbean. Packing for any Caribbean trip takes a bit more time than usual because I must remember to include the gold jewelry and bring the eyelet slips along with the business-related notes and other impedimenta that are a part of my life. First there are meetings at Almond Resorts in Barbados, where I've consulted for more than a decade; then it's off to Guadeloupe for the Fête des Cuisinières. As the only American member of the organization, I must be sure that I shine with my Guadeloupean sisters.

Guadeloupe's annual feast of the women cooks is like nothing else in the region—a day-long celebration of the glories of French-style Creole food. The day begins with a high mass at the cathedral, with all of the members of the Association des Cuisinières and the Mutuel Cuistot: two organizations of cooks and food lovers who are guardians of Guadeloupe's culinary heritage. The women are dressed in full Creole finery made from the fabric selected for the year. Bird of paradise–hued dresses top white eyelet slips starched to a fare-thee-well. It is *de rigeur* to wear copious amounts of gold and so vaults are opened and the assembly decks out in a Queen's ransom of the classic forms—the *chaine forçat* or convict's chain that the slave master gave his slave mistress, the golden balls that were worn when sumptuary laws forbade wearing real pearls, and the ropes of *collier choux* that once signaled the number of children that a nursemaid had raised. Hoop earrings and Madras head ties complete the festive outfits.

Following the mass, the crowd troops through the streets of Pointe à Pitre carrying a statue of St. Lawrence, who is their patron. The grill that is the symbol of his martyrdom—a fitting emblem for a culinary organization—is embroidered on the apron that is worn by all members of the two organizations. The parade ends at a schoolyard where the cooks, their guests, and those fortunate enough to have obtained tickets gather for a lunch that begins with ample rounds of the lime, rum, and sugar cocktail known as a 'ti punch. Preparing one can, at times, take on the intricacy of a Japanese tea ceremony. First there's the sugar, just enough at the bottom of the glass; then a squeeze or two of lime so that the juice moistens the sugar. Muddle it well with your teaspoon, then add a full dose of rum. Too much and you're marked as a drinker; too little and it's limeade. Voila.

Soon, the political speeches are over and the rum has flowed and it's off to the dance floor for an afternoon of dancing to the *beguine* that was at home in the French islands long before Cole Porter heard of it. As the day turns into early evening, the music segues into the drumming of Gros Ka and the more elderly of the ladies head off. Soon, the party is over and it's time to head home to fix another 'ti punch and worry about where to go for dinner.

Barbados: Cane Truck Cogitations

Cane is fierce in Barbados—dense and brutal. Its towering green stalks watch sentinel-like over passing history as it dominates roadsides. Monthly it increases, creating verdant fortresses that slowly grow to blot out the sky. Then in the flash of a cutlass, it disappears to reveal dark, loamy soil pocked with shards and stubble until tender new shoots appear and the cycle begins anew. This is the cane that Richard Ligon must have seen when he stepped forth onto Barbadian shores in 1627 to witness firsthand the birth of the spirit we know as rum.

What madness of conquest drove the British to the Caribbean, we'll only be able to surmise. Certainly if they squinted their eyes against the brutal Caribbean sun, the Barbadian moors of St. Andrew's parish could be mistaken for the northern European ones with which they claimed kinship. But the climate was cruel... even hellish. It burned skin, melted candles, and turned shoes into a mass of mildew and mold. They ignored all in search of money and the wealth that could come from breaking the Spanish and Portuguese monopolies on sugar, and increased their fortunes with their profits made from selling the beverage that would come to be known as rum.

Today's Barbados is different; its booming economy seems to transform more and more acres of sugarcane into condominium dwellings and golf courses. Yet, somehow, as though the cane itself knows that it was the original reason for the island's wealth, it can still grind the newly built multilane super-highway to a screeching halt. In the harvest season, all Bajans know that being stuck behind a cane truck is a thing to be feared. It is guaranteed to make you late for an appointment and, depending on the heat and the level of air-conditioning in the car, it is guaranteed to make you sweat.

If I'm not trying to make a plane back to my northern home, I revel in the way that a seventeenth-century industry can bring the twenty-first to a standstill and sit calmly in the back of my taxi, searching out the allées of royal palms that are the pentimento of former sugar estates. I look for the windmills that turned the crushers and the square chimneys that once belched the sweet smell of burning bagasse from boiling house fires. Being stuck behind a cane truck gives me time to think about the world of rum and of just how it has transformed not only Barbados but also the hemisphere.

Punch au Sirop

makes 1 drink

In the French Antilles, many folks have jars of syrup prepared from tropical fruits on hand to use in cooking and in preparing wonderful punches that have a hint of sunshine. If they don't have time to make them, they can usually pick them up at the market or they'll have the number of an older person who can supply them. I never head home without a jar or two of my favorite passion fruit syrup and perhaps one of *surelles* or *surettes*. They're heavy, but a few spoonfuls go a long way and take me right back to Pointe à Pitre or Fort-de-France. You may use any of the syrup recipes in this book or concoct your own.

1 teaspoon Simple Syrup or Lavender, Ginger, or other syrup (pages 39 to 40)

2 ounces white *rhum agricole*, such as Rhum Damoiseau or Rhum Dillon

Put the syrup in an old-fashioned (bucket) glass or a small wide-mouthed stemmed glass. Pour in the rhum. Stir until well mixed. Serve immediately.

NOTE
Some add an ice cube, but this is considered anathema by many.

Punch à la Noix de Coco

makes 2 drinks

From piña coladas to rum and coconut water, the fruit of the coco palm seems a natural pairing with the elixir of the cane reed. Here is a different twist on the rum and coconut theme—one that can be made in a larger quantity and kept on the sideboard or the bar until ready to serve. It only gets better.

1 cup freshly grated coconut (save the liquid for a different drink if you're grating it yourself)

4 ounces white *rhum agricole*, such as Rhum Dillon

½ cup sugar

2-inch piece vanilla bean

½ teaspoon lemon zest

¼ teaspoon freshly grated nutmeg

Ice cubes (optional)

Coconut slices for garnish (optional)

Put the coconut in a large bowl. Add the rhum and allow it to soak for 1 hour. Strain off the rhum into another bowl. Place the rhum-soaked coconut in a square of cheesecloth and squeeze it into the rhum bowl. Discard the coconut. Add the sugar, vanilla bean, lemon zest, and nutmeg to the bowl. Stir to mix well. Serve over ice and garnish with slices of coconut (if desired).

Banana Punch

makes 1 drink

The banana-boat song and the United Fruit Company notwithstanding, bananas are not originally from the Caribbean region. They may have originated in Malaysia and belong to the same family as the lily and the orchid. The banana turned up in India in the fifth or sixth century BCE in an Indian legend that says that it was the banana, not the apple, that was offered to Adam—a legend that is the reason behind the Latin name for the plantain—*Musa para-disiaca*. Bananas grow in tropical and subtropical climates and are available in many varieties, from the ones with which we are most familiar to small, delicate ones with reddish skins. Any will do for this punch, including the good old Chiquitas.

½ ripe banana (about one 5-inch piece)

4 ounces fresh coconut milk (see page 47)

2 ounces dark Barbadian-style rum, such as Mount Gay Eclipse or Cockspur

2 teaspoons sugar

Ice cubes

Freshly grated nutmeg

Combine the banana, coconut milk, rum, and sugar in a blender and blend until frothy. Pour into an ice-filled glass and top with a few shavings of nutmeg. Serve immediately.

Classic Daiquiri

makes 1 drink

Like many classics in all areas, the daiquiri is simplicity itself. It is a variant on the rum, lime, and sugar theme that is also the hallmark of the 'ti punch of the French islands and the caipirinha of Brazil. There are many stories of the origin of the daiquiri. According to one of them, the daiquiri was invented in the late nineteenth century by two engineers at a copper mine in Oriente Province, Cuba. The miners had company over, but realized too late that nothing remained but rum, limes, and sugar. They named the drink for either the copper mine or the neighboring city of the same name.

Daiquiris became so popular that by the 1930s, Charles Baker in *The Gentleman's Companion* suggested, "A too-sweet daiquiri is like a lovely lady with too much perfume." I concur. But I'm a mere piker with daiquiris when compared with Ernest Hemingway, who drank staggering quantities of them. His preferred watering hole was the Floridita Bar in Havana, where he drank double daiquiris. There, legendary bartender Constante Ribailagua is said to have whipped up more than ten million of them in his life, including the sixteen that Papa Hemingway is said to have consumed in one record-setting session.

2 ounces white rum, such as Bacardi Light or Havana Club

1 ounce freshly squeezed strained lime juice

2 teaspoons Simple Syrup (page 39)

3 to 4 ice cubes

Combine all of the ingredients in a cocktail shaker and shake vigorously. Strain into a chilled martini glass. Serve immediately.

Strawberry Daiquiri

makes 1 drink

Soon after the invention of the home blender, the machines were whirring about turning out all manner of cocktails including a raft of fruit-infused daiquiris. It might seem that strawberries are not Caribbean fruit, but anyone who has traveled to Haiti knows that in Kenskoff in the hills above Port-au-Prince and Petionville, the climate is cool enough to support strawberries and they grow there— small, sweet, and delicious.

½ cup crushed ice

5 large strawberries

2 ounces white rum, such as Bacardi Light

2 teaspoons sugar

½ ounce freshly squeezed strained lime juice

Combine all of the ingredients in a blender and pulse until well mixed and the ice has dissolved. Pour into a large, chilled martini glass. Serve immediately.

Papa Doble

makes 1 hefty drink

Hemingway liked his daiquiris double strength and with a bit of grapefruit juice, and so this Hemingway daiquiri was born.

4 ounces white rum, such as Bacardi Light or Havana Club

2 ounces freshly squeezed strained grapefruit juice

1 ounce freshly squeezed strained lime juice

½ ounce maraschino liqueur

3 or 4 ice cubes

Combine all of the ingredients in a cocktail shaker and shake vigorously. Strain into a large, chilled martini glass. Serve immediately.

Canchanchara

makes 1 drink

This rum, lime juice, and honey drink is also prepared in the French Antilles, where it is known as a *punch au miel.*

2 ounces white rum, such as Bacardi Light

1 ounce freshly squeezed strained lime juice

1 tablespoon honey

Ice cubes

Mix the rum, lime juice, and honey together in a highball glass, stirring to make sure that the honey dissolves. Add ice. Serve immediately.

NOTE
Some folks add a bit of water to lighten the drink.

Mulata

makes 1 drink

This Cuban classic has a decidedly non–politically correct name that allegedly celebrates the charms of Cuban women. I've darkened her up a bit by using two types of rum.

1½ ounces white rum, such as Bacardi Light

½ ounce amber rum, such as Bacardi Gold rum

½ ounce brown crème de cacao

½ ounce freshly squeezed strained lime juice

½ cup crushed ice

Combine all of the ingredients in a blender and pulse until well mixed. Pour into a chilled martini glass. Serve immediately.

Mojito

makes 1 drink

This is one of those Cuban cocktails that is connected to the drinking legend of Papa Hemingway. A small restaurant called La Bodeguita del Medio is where Hemingway drank his, but the drink was also a standby at Sloppy Joe's. Now it's served at bars around the world in infinite varieties.

8 leaves fresh spearmint, plus 1 sprig for garnish

1 ounce freshly squeezed strained lime juice

½ ounce Simple Syrup (page 39)

2 ounces white rum, such as Bacardi Light

Ice cubes

Club soda

Muddle the spearmint leaves, lime juice, and simple syrup in a highball glass. Add the rum and ice and top with club soda. Stir to mix. Garnish with the sprig of spearmint and a straw. Serve immediately.

Mojito a Mi Manera

makes 1 drink

Nothing goes without being changed at my house, so here's the way I really love to make a mojito. It uses ginger syrup, a mix of peppermint and spearmint, and a dash of mint bitters.

4 leaves fresh spearmint, plus 1 sprig for garnish

4 leaves fresh peppermint

1 ounce freshly squeezed strained lime juice

2 teaspoons Ginger Syrup (page 39)

2 ounces white rum, such as Mount Gay Eclipse Silver

Ice cubes

Club soda

Dash of Fee Brothers Mint Bitters (see page 162)

Muddle the mint leaves, lime juice, and ginger syrup in a highball glass. Add the rum and ice and top with club soda and a dash of mint bitters. Stir to mix. Garnish with the sprig of spearmint and a straw. Serve immediately.

Rum Rickey

makes 1 drink

A tall frosted rickey is one of summer's pleasures. This rum rickey combines the usual suspects of rum, lime, and seltzer in a cooling way. Think of it as a mojito without the mint.

2 ounces white rum, such as Mount Gay Eclipse Silver

1 ounce freshly squeezed lime juice, with pulp

Ice cubes

Club soda

Combine the rum and lime juice in a highball glass with ice. Mix gently. Pour in the club soda. Serve immediately.

Rum Swizzle

makes 1 drink

According to Stanley Clisby Arthur, a specialist on the famous beverages of New Orleans, a swizzle is a drink of West Indian origin that probably began in former British Guiana. The name swizzle may be a corruption of "switchel," a Caribbean drink made of molasses and water. The interesting thing here is that enslaved Africans consumed a molasses and water drink in various parts of the hemisphere. It was simply called molasses water in the southern United States and *alua* in Brazil. The swizzle therefore may be a drink that has slave origins. It was popular in the English-speaking Caribbean and eventually made its way to New Orleans.

The most important thing in the preparation of a swizzle is the swizzle stick—a wooden branch from which protrude several smaller sticks like the spokes of a wheel. Swizzle sticks can still be found in markets throughout the Caribbean and are used as whisks. They're called *batons lélé* in the French-speaking islands. Held in the palms of the hands, a swizzle stick is rubbed back and forth, creating a swirling movement that whisks the liquid into a froth. (No swizzle stick? You can use a long bartender's whisk instead.)

2 ounces dark Barbadian-style rum, such as Mount Gay

1 ounce water

1 tablespoon molasses

2 dashes of Peychaud's bitters

Ice cubes

Combine the rum, water, molasses, and bitters in an old fashioned glass. Mix well with a swizzle stick until the mixture froths. Add ice and swizzle again. Serve immediately.

Rum Collins

makes 1 drink

This is a rum variation on the classic Tom Collins. The orange flower water adds an unexpected floral hint to the final drink. Traditionally, the Collins is garnished with a maraschino cherry. This drink is sometimes called a Pedro Collins. Another variant is prepared with a mix of rum and rye whiskey and called a John Collins.

1 ounce freshly squeezed strained lemon juice

½ ounce freshly squeezed strained lime juice

1 teaspoon sugar or Simple Syrup (page 39)

Dash of orange flower water

2 ounces amber rum, such as Old New Orleans Amber or Bacardi Amber

2 ounces club soda

Ice cubes

Combine the juices, sugar, and orange flower water in a Collins or highball glass. Stir well to make sure that the sugar is mixed in. Add the rum and stir to mix, then top with the club soda. Stir a final time and add ice. Serve immediately.

Cuba Libre

makes 1 drink

"Free Cuba" is an intriguing name for a drink that is reputed to go back to before the turn of the twentieth century. It's thought that the sentiment came about at the time of the Spanish-American war. That would make sense and parallel Coca-Cola's rise to fame and fortune. The lime flavor is sometimes enhanced by adding a twist of peel to the glass.

Ice cubes

2 ounces white rum, such as Bacardi Light or Havana Club

½ ounce freshly squeezed strained lime juice

Coca-Cola

1 slice lime

Place ice cubes in a highball glass. Add the rum and lime juice and top with Coke. Stir to mix and garnish with the lime slice. Serve immediately.

Mai Tai

makes 1 drink

After Prohibition, perhaps no one individual did as much for rum drinking as Victor Bergeron. Trader Vic (his nom de guerre) was the owner of a restaurant in Emeryville, California. Legend has it that Tahitian friends of his came in and requested he conjure up something unusual for them. He went to work and, when presented with the finished product, the friends are alleged to have lifted a toast and said, *"Mai tai! Roa ae!"* It is supposed to mean "That is the best thing we've ever had." Another story attributes the creation of the Mai Tai to Don the Beachcomber and suggests that Vic purloined it.

From the 1930s until the 1940s, Trader Vic and Don the Beachcomber controlled empires manned by bartenders who created a repertoire of what are now known as tiki drinks.

1 ounce freshly squeezed strained lime juice

1 ounce Jamaican-style dark rum, such as Myers's or Appleton

1 ounce amber *rhum agricole*, such as Rhum Damoiseau or Rhum St. James

½ ounce orange curaçao

1½ teaspoons Simple Syrup (page 39)

1½ teaspoons orgeat (almond) syrup (see page 36)

Crushed ice

1 sprig peppermint or 1 slice lime between two skewers tied with a twist for garnish

Combine all of the ingredients except the peppermint in a cocktail shaker. Shake vigorously. Strain into a chilled highball glass. Garnish with the peppermint. Traditionally, a Mai Tai is served with a stirrer and a straw.

Bacardi Cocktail

makes 1 drink

Ironically, the Bacardi Cocktail may not be called that in Cuba. The judgment in a 1936 legal case ruled that unless Bacardi rum is used, it is illegal to call this drink a Bacardi Cocktail. There is debate as to whether or not grenadine should be used, but most recipes call for it.

2 ounces white rum, such as Bacardi Light

1 ounce freshly squeezed strained lime juice

1 teaspoon grenadine

Crushed ice

1 maraschino cherry for garnish

Combine the rum, lime juice, and grenadine in a cocktail shaker with crushed ice. Shake vigorously. Strain into a martini glass and garnish with the cherry. Serve immediately.

Cuba's Cocktail Culture

Like Kleenex and Xerox, Bacardi has become a generic term in many parts of the world. The Bacardi distillery, which originated in Cuba, is legendary for its marketing genius, and the family and their product virtually transformed the taste of rum. Even before Prohibition drove thirsty and monied Americans to tropical climes in search of alcohol, Cuba had a strong cocktail culture.

There were three basic types of cocktails that went back to the nineteenth century: *compuestos*, or mixed drinks; *meneaos*, or shaken ones; and *achampanados*, or sparkling drinks. After World War I, Cuba—and Havana in particular—became the world's cocktail mecca. Bartenders from around the globe descended upon the city with some actually transferring their bars with them. Legend has it that a bartender named Donovan transferred his bar lock, stock, and stools from New Jersey, where it was reassembled in the center of Havana as Donovan's. Others attribute similar stories to the establishment known as Sloppy Joe's.

Whatever their origins, the bars of Havana became legendary, with bartenders becoming the princes of the city. Mantaca from Pasaje and Emilio Gonzales from The Florida were two of the first to make reputations for themselves, but soon the bartender dressed in a starched jacket behind a gleaming bar became the norm and the Cuban repertoire of drinks grew. They number such classics as the Presidente (red curaçao, vermouth, and white rum), the Centenario (grenadine, Tia Maria, triple sec, and dark and light rums), and the Isle of Pines (white rum and grapefruit juice).

Folks were still partying on New Year's Eve, when Castro arrived in Havana. He must have understood the value of travel and tourism to the country, because he established a hotel school in 1962 where bartenders are still trained at a long mahogany bar. There, in order to graduate with a top diploma, students had to be able to prepare a minimum of 120 cocktails from memory.

Piña Colada

makes 1 drink

The quintessential rum and coconut drink is the piña colada. Its prime ingredient is cream of coconut, a canned sweetened cream (Coco Lopez is the top of the line). Although the piña colada originated in Puerto Rico, where it was prepared at Schumann's in Viejo San Juan, this piña colada is a salute to the one that I once tasted in the Dominican Republic, where it was prepared from the freshest ingredients possible: fresh pineapple, freshly made coconut milk, and—naturally—fabulous rum. It was served in a hollowed-out pineapple and lives in my taste memory and my dreams. Try one and you'll see why.

1 cup fresh pineapple chunks

2 ounces freshly made coconut milk, chilled (see page 47)

1 ounce dark rum, such as Brugal

1 ounce Dominican-style white rum, such as Bermudez Ron Blanco or Pineapple-Infused Rum (page 106)

3 ice cubes

1 ounce heavy cream

1 wedge pineapple for garnish

Put the pineapple chunks in a blender and pulse until you have a liquid slurry.

Combine ¼ cup of the pineapple liquid, the coconut milk, and both rums in a cocktail shaker with the ice cubes. Add the cream and shake vigorously. Strain into a tall glass and garnish with the pineapple wedge. Serve immediately.

Choco Colada

makes 1 drink

No one knows exactly when coconuts arrived in the Caribbean region. The nuts float and so probably made the transit early on. The tourist image of a coconut palm–fringed beach has become the norm on many of the region's islands. Coconut palm leaves make excellent roofing, coconut logs are sturdy enough to build houses, and the empty shells can be used for bowls and serving vessels. The liquid inside of a green coconut is coconut water. It is pure enough that during World War II, medics in the South Seas were told that in case of shortages, it could be used to replace blood plasma. This is another creamy drink, but one that adds the taste of chocolate instead of pineapple to the mix.

1 ounce white rum, such as Bacardi Light

1 ounce amber rum, such as Bacardi Gold

1 ounce condensed milk

1 ounce cream of coconut

1 tablespoon Hershey's chocolate syrup

Ice cubes

Combine all of the ingredients in a cocktail shaker and stir with a bar spoon until well mixed. Pour into a tall glass and add ice. Serve immediately.

Ponche Crema

makes 4 to 6 drinks

This is a Curaçaoan version of a classic holiday drink consumed in much of the Caribbean region. It is their version of eggnog and is so popular that it is now bottled and sold all year-round.

One 14-ounce can sweetened condensed milk

8 ounces aged rum

4 egg yolks, beaten

1 teaspoon vanilla extract

Combine all of the ingredients in the jar of a blender and process. Pour into a sterilized jar, seal, and keep in the refrigerator until ready to serve.

Coquito

makes 6 to 8 drinks

The word *coquito* means "little coconut" and indeed, coconut milk is the basic ingredient in this deceptively potent punch. It is traditionally served at Christmas celebrations and no *Noche Buena* (Christmas Eve) or *Año Nuevo* (New Year's Eve) would be complete without it.

12 ounces water

3 cinnamon sticks

12 ounces coconut milk

12 ounces evaporated whole milk

12 ounces sweetened condensed milk

12 ounces Puerto Rican–style white rum, such as Bacardi Light

4 egg yolks, well beaten

Ground cinnamon, freshly grated nutmeg, and slivers of toasted coconut for garnishes

Boil the water with the cinnamon sticks for 5 minutes, remove them, and allow the water to cool to room temperature. Combine all of the milks, the rum, and egg yolks in a blender. Add the cinnamon water to taste and blend until you have a frothy liquid. Decant into a sterilized glass bottle, stopper loosely, and refrigerate until ready to serve. To serve, pour into small glasses and top each one with a sprinkle of cinnamon, a grinding of nutmeg, and a sliver of toasted coconut.

Champola

makes 4 drinks

This beverage from Cuba via Puerto Rico is another of those that can be served with or without alcohol. With alcohol, it is a frothy cool punch that is like a soursop milkshake. Without it—well, you decide.

One 8-ounce can soursop nectar

2 cups vanilla ice cream

8 ounces white rum, such as Bacardi Light (optional)

Combine the ingredients in a blender and pulse until smooth. Pour into a stemmed martini glass. Serve immediately.

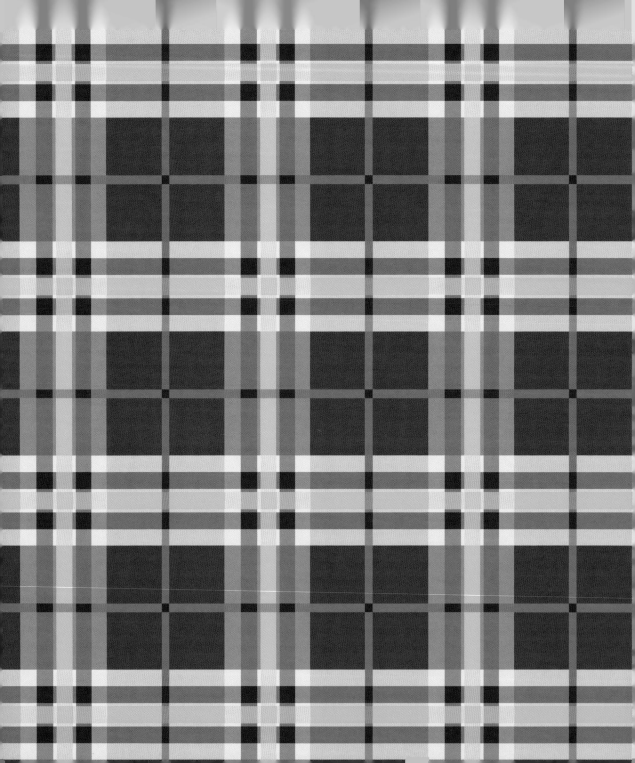

chapter 4

Tropical Tipples

Rum and Ginger

makes 1 drink

For years, I kept a bottle of spicy ginger ale in my refrigerator in anticipation of a visit from my colleague June Bobb. My Guyanese friend was very picky about her rum, so I always had a good selection of that, but she was equally picky about her ginger ale. If you can get Blenheim's ginger ale that comes in three strengths, try this drink with the sharp bite of the extra-strong variety. The rum should be Barbados's Mount Gay. I've recently learned that this drink is also sometimes called a Gin Buck.

Ice cubes

2 ounces dark rum, such as Mount Gay

Spicy ginger ale

1 slice lime

Place ice cubes in a highball glass. Add the rum and ginger ale and stir to mix. Garnish with the lime slice, which can be squeezed into the drink for added zest. Serve immediately.

Tchoupitoulas Street Guzzle

makes 1 drink

There was once a tavern in New Orleans, known as the Iron Horse tavern, that was renowned for its guzzles. There, a similar combination of rum and ginger beer was known as the Tchoupitoulas Street Guzzle. It is similar to the classic Bermudan Dark 'n' Stormy, but has more ginger beer.

6 ounces ginger beer

2 ounces dark rum, such as Gosling's Black Seal

Ice cubes

1 slice lime for garnish

Mix the ginger beer and rum in a tall glass with ice. Garnish with the lime slice. Serve immediately.

Sorrel

makes about 1 quart

Sorrel is what a relative to the hibiscus is called in Jamaica. In the Caribbean, the herb signals Christmas, although it is increasingly consumed year-round. There are many variations on how to prepare this drink; some are heavier on spices and sugar than others. This one is a simple version calling for a bit of cinnamon, cloves, and lots of ginger for zing. It can be served with or without rum. I make my sorrel unsweetened and allow folks to sweeten it themselves with sugar syrup.

1 quart water

3 cups dried sorrel (Roselle) flowers

Two 2-inch cinnamon sticks

Three 2-inch pieces fresh ginger, scraped of peel

8 whole cloves

Simple syrup (page 39)

Dark Barbadian–style rum, such as Mount Gay

Combine the water, sorrel, cinnamon, ginger, and cloves in a large, heavy saucepan and bring to a boil over medium heat. Lower the heat to a simmer and continue to cook for 10 minutes, uncovered. Allow the mixture to cool to room temperature, then strain and decant it into a sterilized quart bottle. Chill the mixture until ready to serve. Pour it into a crystal decanter before serving because the deep pink color is so lovely. Provide simple syrup and rum for guests to add as they like.

Isle of Pines

makes 1 drink

The Isle of Pines off Cuba's southern coast is also called the Island of Youth. This is a tall cooler that is a tribute to the island's cool breezes and fresh atmosphere.

2 ounces white rum, such as Bacardi Light or Havana Club

4 ounces freshly squeezed strained grapefruit juice

Ice cubes

Combine the ingredients in a highball glass and stir with a bar spoon until well mixed. Serve immediately.

Shandy

This is a classic colonial cooler that I've sampled in former British colonies from Bridgetown to Nairobi to New Delhi. It's simply a mix of beer (the local brand is best) with fizzy lemonade. Caribbean beer brands like Caribe, Banks, and Red Stripe are all fine, but if you can't find them, a light local beer like a Budweiser or a Coors will do. The fizzy French lemonade that is sold in many supermarkets is fine.

Caribbean beer

Fizzy French-style lemonade

Ice cubes

1 wedge lemon for garnish (optional)

Mix equal parts of beer and fizzy lemonade in a tall glass over ice. Garnish with the lemon wedge, if desired. Serve immediately.

High-Octane Limeade

makes 4 drinks

This is a refreshing Caribbean drink with limes that can be served either with or without the rum.

4 cups water

8 ounces freshly squeezed strained lime juice

8 ounces dark rum, such as Mount Gay (optional)

2 ounces Lavender Syrup (page 40)

Ice cubes

1 lime, thinly sliced for garnish

Combine the water, lime juice, rum (if using), and lavendar syrup in a large pitcher. Stir until well mixed. Pour into tall glasses filled with ice cubes. Garnish each drink with a lime slice. Serve immediately.

Sangaree

makes 1 drink

West Indian planters lived a rum-soaked life that went from breakfast tipples through luncheon libations, with a break or two for a siesta, then on to evening preprandial drinks. They continued with an array of punches and crystal decanters of liquors during and after dinner, and finished up with a before-bed snort or two before continuing with the same rum-sozzled round the next day. One of the drinks that was often served was Sangaree, a midmorning drink.

8 ounces cold water

1½ ounces dark Barbadian-style rum, such as Mount Gay

1 ounce Madeira wine

½ ounce freshly squeezed strained lime juice

1 teaspoon sugar

Freshly grated nutmeg

Ice cubes

Dash of Angostura Bitters (optional)

Combine the water, rum, Madeira, lime juice, sugar, and a sprinkle of nutmeg in a cocktail shaker. Shake well and pour into a highball glass over ice. Top off with a dash of Angostura Bitters, if desired. Serve immediately.

Rum and Coconut Water

makes 1 drink

I remember back in Harry Belafonte's heyday hearing an old calypso called "Coconut Woman" that stayed with me; it was about drinking rum and coconut water and the effects that the beverage had on the individual. It went: "It could make you very tipsy, make you feel like a gypsy . . . Coco got a lotta iron, make you strong like a lion." At the time, I certainly knew nothing of the delights of demon rum.

     Now, after many trips, when I see a coconut vendor in the very nontropical streets of my Brooklyn neighborhood, I am only too happy to stop and let him swipe the top off of a few coconuts with his machete and pour them into a plastic container so that I can indulge in this perfect tropical pairing. While this can be prepared with the canned coconut water that is readily available, it's best when made with the water from a green coconut that has been freshly topped.

1½ ounces dark Jamaican-style rum, such as Appleton

Ice cubes

2 ounces coconut water (see page 46)

Coconut slices for garnish (optional)

Pour the rum into a chilled highball glass. Add ice and top with the coconut water. Garnish with slices of coconut, if desired. Serve immediately.

Rum Julep

makes 1 drink

In *Famous New Orleans Drinks and How to Mix 'Em*, author Stanley Clisby Arthur suggests that the bourbon-based mint julep might have originated as a rum julep and that the drink arrived in New Orleans in 1793 with refugees from the Haitian Revolution. Get out your silver julep tumblers for this one and frost them in the refrigerator.

4 sprigs fresh peppermint

2 or 3 Demerara sugar cubes

Crushed ice

2 ounces dark rum, such as Rhum Barbancourt 5 Star

Mint bitters (optional; see page 39)

Orange flower water (optional)

1 slice orange (optional)

Strip the leaves from 2 of the peppermint sprigs and place them in the bottom of a bar glass with the sugar. Muddle the sugar and mint leaves with a dash of water. When the mint is well pulverized, pour the mixture into a well-chilled julep tumbler. Add crushed ice and the rhum. Stir to mix well. Garnish with the remaining peppermint sprigs and a straw. Serve immediately. If you want to get fancy, top with a dash of mint bitters and a drop or two of orange flower water and garnish with an orange slice as well as the peppermint.

Rum Daisy

makes 1 drink

Daisies were popular tall drinks in the 1930s. They could be prepared from a range of alcohols. This is a variation on the Santa Cruz Rum Daisy that appears in *The Savoy Cocktail Book*.

2 ounces dark Barbadian-style rum, such as Mount Gay

2 teaspoons Simple Syrup (page 39)

1 teaspoon maraschino liqueur

1 teaspoon freshly squeezed strained lemon juice

Crushed ice

Seltzer water

Combine the rum, simple syrup, maraschino liqueur, and lemon juice in a cocktail shaker. Add crushed ice and shake vigorously. Strain into a highball glass and top with seltzer. Serve immediately.

Shrubb

My friend Maryse says that clementines are traditional in Guadeloupe at Christmastime. People eat them and keep the seeds in their purses and wallets for good luck throughout the year in the same way that some African Americans will keep a black-eyed pea in their pocket for luck and money. This beverage is a way to use all of the clementine, particularly the aromatic peel.

One 1-liter bottle white *rhum agricole*, such as Rhum Damoiseau

Peels from 8 clementines, pith removed, cut into strips

1 whole vanilla bean, split lengthwise

One 3-inch cinnamon stick

3 or 4 whole cloves

Pour off about ½ cup of the rhum from the bottle. You can do this as a holiday libation to the ancestors or just make yourself a 'Ti Punch or two (page 58). Add all of the remaining ingredients to the bottle, pushing the peels down with a chopstick. Cork lightly, and allow it to macerate in the sun for at least 2 weeks. Store in a cool place until ready to serve. You don't have to wait until Christmas! Serve in cordial glasses.

Pimento Rum

makes 1 liter

To the endless confusion of many, allspice berries are referred to as "pimento" in Jamaica. The small round berries are also called Jamaican pepper and have the flavor and scent of a mix of cinnamon, clove, and nutmeg—hence the name allspice. They are the basis for the liqueur that is prepared by Sangster's in Jamaica and called Pimento Dram. This is not as complex as Sangster's mixture, but it is an infusion of allspice berries and other aromatics that makes for a nice after-dinner sipping rum.

One 1-liter bottle amber rum, such as Appleton Estate Special Gold

1 teaspoon allspice berries, crushed

One 4-inch stick cinnamon

1 vanilla bean, split lengthwise

4 whole cloves

⅛ teaspoon freshly grated nutmeg

Pour out about ½ cup of rum and reserve for another use. Add the remaining ingredients to the bottle of rum. Cork lightly and allow it to macerate in the sun for 2 to 3 months. When ready to serve, strain it into a decanter and pour.

Ginger Rum

makes 1 liter

This gingery rum is a perfect addition to drinks you would like with a little kick. It's also wonderful on its own with a splash of soda and a twist of lime.

1 pound fresh ginger, scraped of peel and thinly sliced

1 vanilla bean, split lengthwise

One 4-inch cinnamon stick

One 1-liter bottle white *rhum agricole*, such as Rhum Damoiseau or Rhum Dillon

Simple Syrup (optional; page 39)

Put the ginger, vanilla bean, and cinnamon stick in a large wide-mouth jar and pour in the rhum. Seal it and allow it to macerate in the sun for 2 to 3 months. When ready to serve, taste it and add simple syrup if necessary. Strain into a decanter and serve with a splash of soda and a twist of lime, or use it in other drinks.

Pineapple-Infused Rum

makes 1 liter

Infused rums are a big thing on the island of Guadeloupe, where the tropical fruit is there for the picking and the rum is tinged with the sweet taste of cane. In the national park, the rest stop/bar boasts a wall of glass containers filled with tropical fruits macerating in white rum. These *rhums arrangés*—as they are called—sit and mellow, taking on the flavors of whatever fruits are left in them. An iced-tea jar or *agua fresca* container is perfect for preparing this rum. If you cannot find (or don't wish to use) the more expensive rums from the French islands, this is one place where you can use what Michael Oliviera, my Martha's Vineyard rum purveyor, calls "cost-effective white rum," as even it will take on the tropical tastes.

2 cups fresh pineapple chunks

2 cinnamon sticks

One 1-liter bottle *rhum agricole* or white rum, such as Rhum Damoiseau or Rhum Dillon

Put the pineapple chunks and cinnamon sticks into a large glass container, pour the rhum over and seal it. Allow it to macerate in the sun for 2 to 3 months. The rum will mellow and take on the flavor of the pineapple, creating your own special pineapple rum. When ready, discard the fruit and serve as an after-dinner drink in a cordial glass or use in piña coladas in place of the white rum.

Spiced Rum

makes 1 liter

On my last official trip to Almond Resorts in Barbados, I was surprised to notice a new jar on the bar. It was filled with spices and radiated with a rich deep color. It was spiced rum. The company had acquired two properties in St. Lucia a few years back, and the St. Lucian employees were making a spiced rum that caught on with the guests. Soon the Almond Resorts in Barbados were making their own variations of spiced rum. This is one version; the trick is to improvise until you have one that perfectly suits your tastes.

One 1-liter bottle white Barbadian-style rum, such as Mount Gay

6 maraschino cherries and 2 tablespoons of their liquid

3 bay leaves

5 whole cloves

One 5-inch cinnamon stick

7 allspice berries, cracked

½ teaspoon cracked black peppercorns

Combine all of the ingredients in a large jar and cover loosely. Allow the spiced rum to sit for at least 2 weeks. When ready to drink, strain it into a decanter and serve sparingly in small cordial glasses, or use it instead of your regular rum in a Rum and Coke.

Rasta Rum

makes ½ gallon

I discovered this trick at the American Airlines lounge at the Puerto Rican airport. There they have a beautiful glass jar with a spigot, filled to the top with this mix. I now have a similar glass jar with a spigot, and occasionally throw a party with enough folks to enjoy a gallon or two of the stuff. The trick is to have a jar where the beauty of the floating peppers can be seen and where the spigot allows you to serve it out as you wish. I call it Rasta Rum because the red, green, and yellow bell peppers are the Rasta colors.

2 red bell peppers

2 green bell peppers

2 yellow bell peppers

2 jalapeño chiles

1 habanero chile

One 4-ounce can jalapeño-stuffed olives, drained

½ gallon cost-effective white rum

Arrange the whole bell peppers, chiles, and olives in a 1-gallon jar. Pour the rum over them. Allow the mixture to macerate in the sun for at least 2 weeks before using. The bell peppers give a delicate je ne sais quoi flavor to the rum that also takes on the heat of the chiles. Serve with a twist of lemon in a spicy Rum Bloody Mary (page 111).

For a quick version: Slice the peppers; macerate for at least 2 days or up to 1 week.

Yellowbird

makes 1 drink

This is named for the song that virtually became the Caribbean national anthem. "Yellowbird," as sung by Harry Belafonte, is an English-language version of a folk song from Haiti known as "Choucoune." Yellowbird the drink is deceptive. Be careful—one too many and the yellowbird will not be the only thing high up in the banana tree.

2 ounces freshly squeezed strained orange juice

1 ounce freshly squeezed strained lime juice

1 ounce white rum, such as Mount Gay

1 ounce dark rum, such as Appleton

1½ teaspoons Tia Maria

Crushed ice

1 sprig fresh mint for garnish

Combine the juices, rums, and Tia Maria in a cocktail shaker with crushed ice. Shake vigorously. Strain into a highball glass half-filled with crushed ice. Garnish with the mint sprig. Serve immediately.

Rum Bloody Mary

makes 1 drink

The taste of sugarcane and the sweetness of molasses that are undercurrents in all rum seem to complement sweeter drinks rather than savory ones. This drink is therefore a surprising twist on the traditional Bloody Mary, using white rum infused with bell peppers and chiles, that will make a convert of you. As with all of my Bloody Marys—whether prepared with rum or the more traditional vodka—I like it very spicy and with the conceit of a pickled okra pod as garnish.

4 ounces tomato juice

2 ounces Rasta Rum (page 108) or white rum, such as Bacardi Light

½ ounce freshly squeezed strained lemon juice

1 teaspoon Worcestershire sauce

¼ teaspoon celery salt

¼ teaspoon Tabasco sauce

Prepared horseradish sauce

Freshly ground black pepper

2 ice cubes

1 spicy pickled okra pod for garnish

Combine the tomato juice, rum, lemon juice, Worcestershire, celery salt, Tabasco, and horseradish and pepper to taste in a cocktail shaker with ice cubes and shake well. Taste and adjust the seasonings as needed. Strain into a chilled stemmed glass and garnish with the pickled okra pod. Serve immediately.

Boa Noite

makes 1 drink

This is a simple mixture that is guaranteed to put you to sleep with a smile, hence the name, which simply means "good night" in Portuguese. I came up with this mixture one evening with some friends, when we just wanted to relax and have one last drink before evening's end. The slightly tart taste of the passion fruit perfectly complements the rum and the result is a great way to end any evening.

1½ ounces Mount Gay Sugarcane rum

Ice cubes

4 ounces passion fruit juice

Pour the rum over ice cubes in an old-fashioned glass and top with the passion fruit juice. Serve immediately.

Green Flash

makes 1 drink

The green flash is the last flare of light at sunset as the fiery orb disappears into the water. For years I thought it was just another of those hoary legends that old hands torture newbies with. Then on a cruise, while indulging in a preprandial sip or two at an outside lounge, I was startled and then delighted to actually see the green flash. It was amazing! When I got back Stateside, I decided to celebrate with the creation of this concoction celebrating the green wonder.

2 ounces white rum, such as Mount Gay

2 ounces freshly squeezed strained grapefruit juice

1 ounce passion fruit juice

½ ounce blue curaçao

Ice cubes

Club soda

1 wedge grapefruit for garnish

Combine the rum, juices, and curaçao in a cocktail shaker with ice. Shake vigorously. Strain into a highball glass and top with club soda and garnish with a grapefruit wedge on a skewer. Serve immediately.

Rum Toddy

makes 1 drink

Even in the tropical Caribbean region, a sick person is often put to bed with a hot toddy to sweat out a cold. This is a simple version of the medicinal beverage that can double as a winter warmer for those of us in more northern climes. You will need a heatproof mug.

4 ounces hot water

2 ounces dark rum, such as Mount Gay

2 teaspoons freshly squeezed strained lemon juice

2 teaspoons freshly squeezed strained lime juice

1 teaspoon sugar

3 whole cloves, crushed

Combine all the ingredients in a heatproof mug or Irish Coffee glass and stir well until the sugar dissolves. Serve immediately and drink while hot.

Navy Grog

makes 1 drink

Admiral Edward Vernon is the man responsible for diluting the rum ration that was given to the sailors in the British Navy, when he found that the rum was contributing to numerous accidents on board. Vernon was affectionately known by his sailors as "Old Grosgram" for the waterproof cloak that he wore. In short time, the drink became known by shortening that nickname to grog.

For years, the British Virgin Island firm of Pusser's was one of the many companies that supplied the rum to the British Navy. The grog drinking that Vernon established endured until July 31, 1970, known as Black Tot Day. Grogs can be served hot or chilled.

2 ounces dark rum, such as Pusser's

2 ounces boiling water

1 teaspoon freshly squeezed strained lime juice

Combine the ingredients in an Irish Coffee glass and stir. Serve immediately.

Jamaican Coffee

makes 1 drink

While hot drinks are not usually associated with the Caribbean, this after-dinner drink is a good way to close out the evening. You will need a heatproof glass like an Irish Coffee glass.

2 tablespoons Caribbean Spiced Sugar (page 41)

1½ ounces Jamaican-style dark rum, such as Appelton, plus more for rimming

1 ounce Tia Maria

4 ounces hot black Jamaican coffee

Whipped cream

Put the spiced sugar in a saucer. Rub the edge of a heatproof glass with rum and then place it upside down on the saucer to coat the rim of the glass with the sugar. Slowly pour the 1½ ounces rum and the Tia Maria into the glass and add the coffee. Top with whipped cream. Serve immediately.

Jamaican Rafting

Port Antonio is my favorite spot in Jamaica. Lush, green, and quiet, it lacks the glitz of Ocho Rios and gets along quite nicely, thank you very much, without the madness of Negril. For years, it figured largely in my fantasy life for two reasons: a hotel named Trident and rafting on the Rio Grande.

Trident was a grand hotel in the Jamaican style of the past, with the hallmarks of English baronial splendor coupled with Jamaican décor. The rooms were at water's edge and salt spray dampened the chintz-covered chaise lounges. A pair of white peacocks strolled the grounds and added to the otherworldly air. Service was impeccable, with the bar manned by a mixologist from whom rum kept no secrets. He produced drinks with a flourish and a flair: rum punches, planter's punches, daiquiris, and more. In the evening, a pianist entertained in the library before dinner and conversation was appropriately international and terribly sophisticated. The hotel evoked the Jamaica of times past when Noel Coward and Ian Fleming could be found at cocktail parties and Errol Flynn lived on Navy Island out in the Port Antonio Harbor.

Errol Flynn is said to be the creator of my second favorite thing about Port Antonio. It is thought that he was the first to take his guests out on the bamboo and wood rafts that had previously been used to transport bananas down the Rio Grande to the ships waiting at port. Rafting has now become one of the island's tourist attractions and it is one of my favorite things to do in Jamaica.

The beauty of rafting is that there is nothing to do but sit back with a tall rum drink in hand and enjoy the quiet and calm of nature as you are poled down the river. The water is cool and the arches of greenery overhead dapple the sunlight. The only sounds are the rhythmic splashes of the rafter's pole as he propels you gondolierlike through the current. The rafters occasionally fancy themselves singers and a verse or two of Marley is not out of place, but usually I am happy to savor the silence and look for the next rest spot, where I can get a taste of some jerk and a refill of my rum drink before continuing the journey down the river.

Returning to Trident after a day of rafting is my idea of true bliss. The hotel and the activity mark the dueling sides of my personality. Trident appeals to my love of luxury and wish to bask in the glories of good service and rafting appeals to my love of nature's calm. As are many things in life, both are immensely enhanced by a glass or two of very good rum.

Hurricane

makes 1 drink

I'm not sure why they haven't changed the name of this beverage post–Hurricane Katrina, but these drinks are some of the most popular cocktails ever in the Crescent City. The place to imbibe is Pat O'Brien's, which has been described as the city's ultimate party bar—and in New Orleans that's saying a lot!

Legend has it that during Prohibition, a nearby speakeasy was accessed by uttering the words, "storm's a-brewing." If indeed the storm was a liquid hurricane, the classic hurricane glass—a tall curved one—resembles the lanterns that used to be placed over candles to keep them from guttering during the strong hurricane winds, hence the name. Pat O'Brien's sells its own mix; this is my variation of the classic drink.

2 ounces dark rum, such as Appleton

1 ounce white rum, such as Mount Gay

1 ounce freshly squeezed strained lime juice

1 ounce fresh pineapple juice

1 ounce freshly squeezed strained orange juice

½ ounce Rose's Lime Juice

1½ teaspoons passion fruit syrup (see page 162)

Crushed ice

1 orange wedge for garnish

1 maraschino cherry for garnish

Combine the rums, juices, and syrup in a cocktail shaker with a scoop of crushed ice. Shake vigorously. Strain into a hurricane glass half-filled with crushed ice. Garnish with the orange wedge, cherry, and a straw. Serve immediately.

Corn and Oil

makes 1 drink

Barbados is a small island, and there seems to be a church on every corner. What is even more astonishing is that there seems to be at least one rum shop for every church! Specialists in the art of hospitality since the seventeenth century, Barbadians know how to be welcoming. While the women go to church, the men often adjourn to the small shacks where the members of the "bar association" convene to fire off a few Corn and Oils. Barbadians like their drinks sweet; I cut some of the sweetness with a twist of lime.

2 ounces Barbadian-style or other white rum, such as Mount Gay

1½ teaspoons Falernum (page 41)

Ice cubes

Mix together the rum and Falernum in a cocktail shaker. Pour over ice in a highball glass. Serve immediately.

Mojitos with Papa in Cuba

Cuba looms on the horizon for any lover of the Caribbean. While I'm not old enough to have bellied up to the bar at Sloppy Joe's in the Batista days, I did visit the island in the days when Fidel was still making day-long speeches in the Plaza de la Independencia. It was back in the days of the Carter presidency when, for a few brief moments, travel to Cuba was legal for all Americans. I went with a group that stayed at the former Hilton and we traveled through the country.

Cuba was a marvel for me. Upon exiting the aircraft and the terminal, I looked around and realized that Cuba was indeed a Caribbean nation and a huge one at that, with a large African cultural component and a huge brown-skinned population. I was amazed that there were masses of people who looked just like my relatives and me, and it was a shock. The size of this country was a marvel to me, and its capital city, although showing signs of its age, offered hints of its glorious past and its former cosmopolitan sophistication. I also understood the fierce love of country of all *Cubanos* because it is truly a beautiful place.

Cuba's tourism plant had not ramped up to the international traffic that the island now hosts and so sightseeing consisted of drives through old neighborhoods in Havana, walking around the plazas, and visiting Hemingway's home, *la Finca Vigia*. Located about twelve miles outside of Havana, the home was kept as a shrine to Papa Hemingway and we stood outside of the windows on the steps provided

and peeked in voyeurlike at the house. We peered at the spines of books looking for hints of sources, mentally catalogued the liquors on the bar, and smiled conspiratorially at the notations of weight and blood pressure written on the bathroom walls.

Later on the trip we found other evidence of Hemingway's preferences at a small restaurant wallpapered with business cards, where we were served a simple, yet delicious meal of pork with black beans and white rice. It was *La Bodeguita del Medio*, home of one of Hemingway's favorite cocktails, the mojito. I recall sipping my first one and being charmed. I watched carefully as they were prepared and took note when the bartender reminded all that it was prepared with *yerba buena* (similar to spearmint—not peppermint, as many use). This was my kind of drink and it even came with a pedigree. I immediately added it to my list of Caribbean favorites along with the 'Ti Punch that had won my heart in Guadeloupe. Later in the trip, we would visit *La Floridita*, where Hemingway met the daiquiri for the first time and there, too, I would be charmed. But "the little shop in the middle," as La Bodeguita's name translates, had a local flair and neighborhood flavor that the grander establishment didn't. Perhaps it's my love of pork and black beans, or perhaps it's the warmth of the bartender and knowing the mint hint, but next time I'm in Havana, I'll be taking my mojito at La Bodeguita with Papa's ghost.

Zombie

makes 1 drink

Named for Haiti's Voodoo undead, who are fodder for horror movies and late-night tall tales, this drink packs a wallop. The question about its name is whether it transforms the drinker into a zombie or requires that you be one to survive the concoction! Properly speaking, it is not a Caribbean cocktail, but rather one of the tiki drinks created by legendary bartender Ernest Raymond Beaumont-Gantt, better known to the drinking world as Don the Beachcomber.

1 ounce white rum, such as Bacardi Light

1 ounce amber rum, such as Appleton Estate Special Gold

1 ounce dark rum, such as Mount Gay

½ ounce maraschino liqueur

1 ounce pineapple juice

1 ounce freshly squeezed strained lime juice

1 ounce freshly squeezed strained lemon juice

1 ounce passion fruit syrup (page 162)

Crushed ice

151-proof dark rum, such as Bacardi

1 wedge pineapple for garnish

1 sprig fresh mint for garnish

Combine all of the ingredients except the 151 rum and garnishes in a cocktail shaker with a scoop of crushed ice. Shake vigorously and strain into a highball glass. Float a spoonful of 151 rum on top by slowly pouring it over the back of a spoon into the glass. Garnish with the pineapple wedge, mint sprig, and a straw. Serve immediately.

Last Call in New Orleans

The Crescent City on the Mississippi is a place that has adopted me. While I'd love to claim that it's the other way around, it's clear that the city has captured and indeed captivated me.

I knew I was a goner on my first trip there in the 1970s when I managed a dinner at Dooky Chase's; attended a knock-down, drag-out party with newly made friends; and joined the second line at a jazz funeral all in one weekend. And that was only the beginning. In the intervening years, I've made friends who I now count as family, found a second academic home amid the venerable oaks of Dillard University, own my very own Creole cottage, and have my own vast and growing collection of cocktail tales to tell.

Perhaps the most poignant is my own last call. In July of 2005, I was asked to be the keynote speaker for the Southern Foodways Alliance's field trip that was to be held in my city. I normally don't let July catch me in the overheated town. For the SFA though, I made an exception and was hanging out, sampling the chef's offerings and sweating with friends at the opening party that was held in the distillery where Cane rum, New Orleans's very own, was made and sold. I stopped off in the gift shop to purchase a bottle or two and put them aside. The next day it was lectures and liveliness, calas, Creole cream cheese, and cane.

It all came to a screeching halt when I got home and looked at the television—a hurricane was brewing in the Gulf of Mexico. I changed plane reservations and rapidly performed my usual lockdown activities that accompany my annual northern migration. All of this was done to the accompaniment of my friends' laughter at my cowardice. They were right, it wasn't Katrina; it was Dennis, one of the earlier storms that buffeted the Gulf in 2005. Later in the summer in the North, I watched in horror as Katrina came ashore at Waveland, Mississippi, and the next day as water flooded my city.

I was one of the fortunate ones; my house survived not only that earlier storm but also the devastation that the combination of Hurricane Katrina and the Army Corps of Engineers produced. When I returned to New Orleans in November of that year, it was a place transformed. A New Orleanian friend of mine has threatened to get a bar code tattoo that says Best Before August 29, 2005. I concur, but I take heart in watching my adopted home show its mettle and reveal spunk and heart.

The Cane distillery didn't survive the flood and as I drove the trail of high water with my friends upon my return, we stopped and I watched in horror at the dirty stain of a watermark that scarred it. My two bottles of Cane rum ironically did survive and some day I will open them. I'll assemble my New Orleans family from their various far-flung post-Katrina new homes, pour some of the rum on the ground to appease and sweeten the souls of those who didn't make it, and prepare some hurricanes from the mellow rum. We'll lift a glass to my city at the bend in the river, knowing that the last call for my city is a long, long way off.

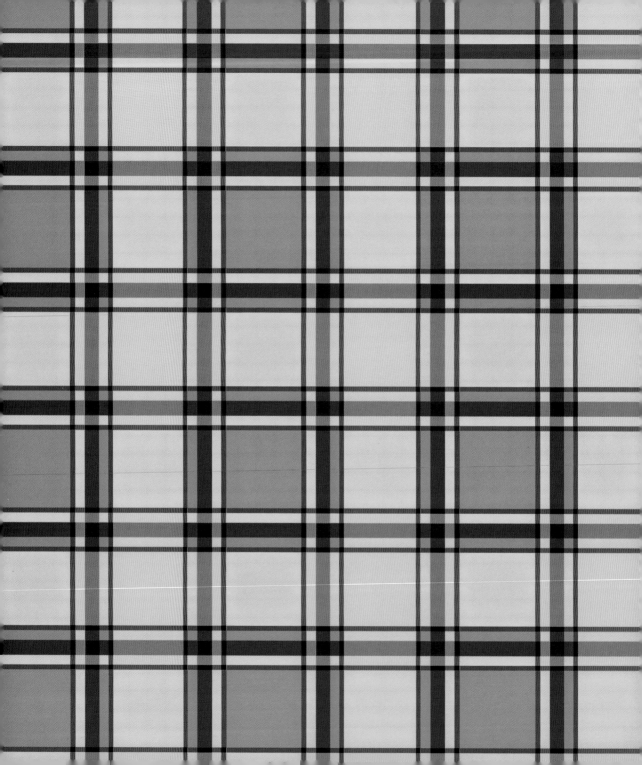

chapter 5

Caribbean Snacks

Plantain Chips

Why buy those plantain chips in a bag when with very little effort you can make your own and have them fresh and seasoned to your taste? The big brothers of the banana family are readily available in most supermarkets and can always be found in Hispanic or Caribbean neighborhoods. You can create your own flavors by adding savory spices like pimentón (smoked paprika) or chili powder, or sweet with the addition of cinnamon and brown sugar.

Vegetable oil, for frying

3 large green plantains

Salt

Hot pimentón, chili powder, cinnamon, and sugar, or other seasonings (optional)

Heat 2 inches of oil to 375°F in a heavy Dutch oven or deep fryer. Cut the plantains into ¼-inch rounds. Drop the plantains into the oil in small batches and fry until browned and crisp, turning once, 2 to 3 minutes total. When the chips are done, fish them out with a slotted spoon and drain them on paper towels. When they are all dry, place them in a paper bag with salt and seasonings (if using) to taste and shake to coat them with the mixture. Serve warm to accompany drinks.

NOTE

Green plantains will stain your hands when you peel them. To avoid this, either slather your hands with cooking oil before peeling or peel the plantains under cold water.

Coconut Crisps

serves 6 to 8

I first tasted these chips on Navy Island, a small island in the harbor of Port Antonio, Jamaica. Navy Island was once the home of actor Errol Flynn. When I visited, his home had been transformed into a series of small bungalows that could be rented and were accessible only via a small skiff that brought visitors out to the island. In the evening, rather than head off-island into the small club in town, my friends and I sat around and enjoyed rum punches with the coconut crisps that are perfect accompaniments to Caribbean drinks. The hardest part of this is preparing the coconut.

1 brown coconut

Salt

Open the coconut by placing it in a 350°F oven for 10 minutes. Remove it to a hard surface and whack it solidly with a hammer along the fault lines that have formed. Drain the liquid, then use a dull knife to pry the coconut meat away from the shell. Peel the white coconut meat into long thin strips with a potato peeler, grater, or mandoline.

Preheat the broiler. Place the coconut strips on a cookie sheet and brown them under the broiler until they are lightly toasted and crisp, 2 to 3 minutes. Watch carefully because they can go from a delicate brown to a black char in a second or two of inattention. Salt lightly. Serve immediately with cocktails.

Bacon-Wrapped Pickled Watermelon

makes 24 pieces

My friend Chef Ken Smith, who is the executive chef of the Upperline restaurant in New Orleans, created this appetizer. It's a fanciful Southern take on the bacon-wrapped water chestnuts and chicken livers that appeared on the flaming pupu platters of tiki restaurant fame. Here, they take on a sweet Southern flavor. You can make your own watermelon-rind pickles. In that case, I refer you to your grandmother's recipe, or you can use store-bought pickled rind and no one will be the wiser.

12 strips bacon, cut in half crosswise

24 one-inch pieces watermelon-rind pickle

Soak 24 toothpicks in water for a half hour so that they won't burn during cooking. Preheat the broiler. Wrap the bacon strips around the watermelon pickle pieces and secure with the toothpicks. Place them on a broiling pan or cookie sheet with sides (the bacon will render its fat as it cooks and you don't want it to run all over your broiler). Place the pan under the broiler and cook, turning the pieces once, until the bacon is crisped, about 5 minutes. Serve immediately.

Pumpkin Fritters with Raisins

Frituras de Calabaza con Pasas

makes about 12 fritters

This pumpkin fritter is one of Cuba's variations on Caribbean fritters. It is a savory fritter, but the raisins give a hint of sweetness that goes well with rum drinks. Be sure to use calabaza—West Indian cooking pumpkin—or you can substitute acorn squash.

2 tablespoons raisins

1¼ cup dark Jamaican-style rum, such as Appleton

12 ounces calabaza, peeled, seeded, and cut into 2-inch pieces

1 teaspoon all-purpose flour

2 large eggs

Salt

Freshly ground black pepper

Vegetable oil, for frying

Put the raisins in a small bowl and cover with the rum. Allow the raisins to plump at room temperature for 2 hours.

Put the calabaza in a medium saucepan with water to cover. Bring to a boil, then lower the heat and simmer for 15 minutes, or until the squash is fork tender. Drain the squash, place it in a bowl, and mash it with a potato masher or a fork until it is a smooth puree. Sprinkle the flour over the calabaza and mix it in well. Beat the eggs and add them to the mixture, stirring to make sure that they are mixed in well. Drain the raisins (drink the rum if you wish) and add them to the bowl. Continue to mix. Season with salt and pepper.

Heat 2 inches of oil to 375°F in a medium skillet. Drop in teaspoons of the fritter mixture, frying until the fritters are golden brown, about 5 minutes. Remove with a slotted spoon, drain on paper towels, and repeat until all of the mixture is fried. Serve immediately.

Toasted Cashews

serves 4 to 6

Ever since I first saw cashew fruit growing in the Caribbean, and realized that there's only one little question mark of a nut hanging at the tip of each fruit, I've understood why the slightly sweet nuts are so expensive. They're another addition to my party repertoire and I season them up with a dash of chili powder—the kind that is a mix of chiles with a hint of cumin.

1½ tablespoons butter

2 cups cashew nuts

1 teaspoon salt

2 teaspoons Mexican chili powder

In a heavy skillet over medium heat, melt the butter. Sauté the cashews until lightly browned, 5 to 7 minutes. Stir occasionally to make sure that the nuts do not burn. Remove the nuts and drain them on paper towels. Place the salt and chili powder in a brown paper bag, add the nuts, and shake the bag to coat them well. Serve warm with cocktails.

Spicy Fried Chickpeas

Channa

serves 4 to 6

This is one of my favorite kinds of recipes—so simple it almost doesn't merit being called a recipe. It can be prepared using dried chickpeas that have been soaked overnight in water and will have a bit more crunch, but these are just fine by me. They're sold throughout the English-speaking Caribbean under the name of *channa*. They originated in Trinidad, where there is a significant Indian population.

One 1-pound can whole chickpeas (Goya is a good brand)

Salt

Cayenne pepper

Preheat the broiler. Drain the chickpeas and spread them on a cookie sheet with sides. Season them with salt and cayenne. Place them under the broiler stirring occasionally until they are browned and crunchy, 3 to 5 minutes. Serve warm.

NOTE
You can vary the flavor of your *channa* by playing around with ingredients like pimentón (smoked paprika) or other powdered chilies.

Puerto Rican Corn Fritters

Surrulitos

makes about 10

These cornmeal and cheese fritters are a part of the Puerto Rican culinary tradition of *cuchifritos*—tasty fried tidbits that are perfect for snacking. They make great appetizers and are perfect with drinks.

1½ cups yellow cornmeal

1¼ cups hot water

½ teaspoon salt

½ cup grated *queso blanco* or other soft white cheese

Vegetable oil, for frying

Stir the cornmeal, water, and salt together in a medium saucepan. Cook over low heat, stirring constantly, until a thick mush forms. Add the cheese and stir to incorporate. Allow the mixture to cool to room temperature, then shape it into thumb-size ovals.

Heat 2 inches of oil to 375°F in a heavy fryer or Dutch oven. Drop in the surrulitos a few at a time and fry until golden brown on both sides, turning once, about 5 minutes. Remove with a slotted spoon and drain on paper towels. Serve immediately.

Sugarcane Shrimp

makes 12 skewers

These skewers of marinated barbecued shrimp are pure cocktail fun because you get to eat the sugarcane skewers as well. The cane gives the shrimp a subtle sweetness and everyone loves to suck on the skewers after the shrimp are but a memory.

12 large fresh shrimp, peeled and deveined

⅓ cup freshly squeezed lime juice

⅓ cup low-sodium soy sauce

1 tablespoon dark Jamaican-style rum, such as Appleton

1 tablespoon olive oil

1 teaspoon Demerara sugar

¼ teaspoon minced garlic

Salt

Freshly ground black pepper

Minced habanero chile (substitute jalapeño for a milder taste)

24 two-inch chunks fresh pineapple

12 eight-inch sugarcane skewers (see note)

Wash the shrimp and place them in a large bowl. Combine the lime juice, soy sauce, rum, oil, sugar, and garlic in a second bowl. Season with salt, pepper, and habanero. Pour the liquid over the shrimp. Cover with plastic wrap and allow the shrimp to marinate while preheating the broiler. When

continued ...

ready, thread 1 pineapple chunk, 1 shrimp, then a second pineapple chunk on each skewer. Place the skewers on a broiler pan and cook until lightly browned, turning once, 3 to 5 minutes. When done, serve the Sugarcane Shrimp on their skewers on a platter while hot.

NOTE

To make sugarcane swizzle sticks and skewers, wash the sugarcane stalk thoroughly. Using a sharp chef's knife, carefully cut the stalk crosswise, at a joint, into sections the length of the skewer needed. Be careful, as the cane is harder than you think. Split at the center of the core lengthwise into quarters for 4 skewers. Don't remove the outer bark; it reinforces the skewer. Sharpen the ends of the skewers into points.

Soused Cucumbers

serves 6

This salad is like the one that my mother used to make every summer. Just seeing a cucumber and smelling the almost violet perfume of a really fresh one makes me think of this cooling slurry of slippery cuke and onion. Here the Caribbean touch is the heat of the habanero with the cool cucumber.

3 large cucumbers, peeled and thinly sliced

2 medium Vidalia onions, thinly sliced

¼ cup cane vinegar (see page 162)

¼ cup freshly squeezed lime juice

1 tablespoon water

1 teaspoon brown sugar

¼ teaspoon minced habanero chile, or to taste

Salt

Freshly ground black pepper

Alternately layer the sliced cucumbers and onions in a medium glass bowl. Whisk together the remaining ingredients in a small bowl. Taste and adjust seasoning with salt and pepper. Pour the mixture over the cucumbers and onions. Cover the bowl with a plate that fits inside it, weight the plate with a 1-pound can, and refrigerate for 3 hours. When ready to serve, remove the weight and plate, fluff the cucumbers and onions with a fork, and serve chilled.

Janga

Traditionally, these are small shrimp that can be found in the rivers of Jamaica. They are caught and peppered and find their way onto the menus at the pork pits that dot the country's touristy north coast. They can also occasionally be found in the small stands that have sprung up along the country's rivers, where rafting is a popular pastime. They are sold in plastic bags and are perfect for nibbling. As janga are impossible to find in this country, I have substituted small shrimp.

2 cups distilled white vinegar

1 tablespoon finely minced onion

1 garlic clove, minced

4 allspice berries, crushed

¼ teaspoon minced Scotch Bonnet chile, to taste

Salt

Freshly ground black pepper

1 pound small shrimp, peeled, deveined, and cooked

Combine the vinegar, onion, garlic, allspice, and chile in a small non-reactive saucepan. Season with salt and pepper and bring to a boil. Lower the heat and allow the mixture to simmer until the onion softens, stirring occasionally, 2 to 3 minutes.

Put the shrimp in a heatproof wide-mouthed crock or bowl. Pour the hot marinade over the shrimp, cover with plastic wrap, and refrigerate for at least 12 hours. When ready to serve, stir the shrimp, drain them, and serve chilled.

Dominican Fried Chicken

Chicharrónes de Pollo

serves 6

These small chicken bits are so popular in the Dominican Republic that they can almost be considered the national dish.

One 2- to 3-pound frying chicken or chicken parts

¼ cup freshly squeezed lime juice

1 tablespoon ginger soy sauce

1 tablespoon dark Jamaican-style rum, such as Appleton

1 teaspoon minced garlic

1 teaspoon dark brown sugar

1 teaspoon salt

Vegetable oil, for frying

1 cup all-purpose flour

½ teaspoon paprika

1 teaspoon freshly ground black pepper

Cut the chicken into small pieces by dividing the wings, thighs, and legs into halves and the breasts into quarters. In a large bowl, whisk together the lime juice, soy sauce, rum, garlic, sugar, and salt. Add the chicken pieces to the marinade. Cover and refrigerate for at least 4 hours.

Heat 2 inches of oil to 375°F in a heavy skillet. Put the flour, paprika and pepper in a paper bag. Drop in the chicken pieces a few at a time and shake to coat. Gently place a few of the chicken pieces in the hot oil and fry on each side until cooked through and golden brown, 7 to 8 minutes. Do not crowd the skillet, or the oil will cool and the frying will take longer. Remove the chicken with a slotted spoon and drain on paper towels. Repeat until all the pieces are fried. Serve immediately.

The Three Bs of the Dominican Republic

In the 1980s, if it was Saturday night in Santo Domingo, it was time to be on the Malecón—the local name for the Avenida George Washington that parallels the sea. During the day it was home to some of the city's fanciest hotels and boutiques; when the sun went down, it was transformed into the world's longest open-air merengue party every weekend. It was intoxicating. Cars parked along the strip with their windows rolled down and their music turned up—"celebrating the feast of Saint Radio" as my cousin called it. Each car had its own sound system with its graphic equalizer working overtime and its own selection of music, so as you walked the strip one set of tunes segued into another, but the infectious beat transformed the cacophony into a not unpleasant whole.

The warm air was comfortable and the occasional breeze from the water kept it from getting too hot. Interspersed among the cars were trucks selling nibbles that could be consumed while walking. Best of all there were folks with coolers offering small tastes of one of the island's three Bs and mixers.

The three Bs of the Dominican Republic are quite simply the island's three favorite brands of rum: Brugal, Barcelo, and Bermudez. Each has its partisans, but I wasn't picky; I drank whatever came out of the cooler. It was all good and I knew that I just wanted the music not to stop and to keep dancing my way down the Malecón.

When I was in the Dominican Republic to write a guidebook section, the Malecón was definitely my favorite weekend hangout, but I also learned to love the island's north coast. Years ago, outside of Cabarete, I found one of my dream Caribbean beaches and tasted the best piña colada I've ever had. The beach was pristine; only a small shack for changing transformed it from what it must have been when the Admiral of the Seas arrived in 1492—palm trees lined the white sand. The water was the turquoise that seems to exist only in travel posters. And the best thing of all—it was deserted. I was the only person on the beach except for two young boys who offered to make me a piña colada. Naturally, I stopped and thought that if they were game, so was I, so I purchased one . . . and it was sublime. It was prepared in a coconut shell from freshly crushed pineapple and freshly prepared coconut milk—no fancy bar tools, no blender rattling around, just pure simplicity. The taste was perfect: the combination of the slightly acidic sweetness of the fresh pineapple and the nuttiness of the coconut.

I've never been back to that beach; it's probably crowded and filled with refreshment stands and I haven't merengued on the Malecón in more than a decade, but when I shut my eyes and sip the piña coladas that I have learned to prepare in the same way, I'm back in the Dominican Republic, savoring the island's three Bs.

Caribbean-Style Deviled Eggs

makes 24 pieces

Folks in the French Caribbean have their own way with deviled eggs. Try these when you're entertaining. In a pinch, you can substitute tuna instead of the crabmeat, but they will not be the same.

12 hard-boiled eggs

3 tablespoons mayonnaise

2 tablespoons fresh lump crabmeat, picked and flaked

1 tablespoon Dijon mustard

¼ teaspoon Mexican chili powder

¼ teaspoon hot pimentón or hot paprika, plus extra for garnish

Salt

Freshly ground black pepper

Gently peel then slice each egg in half lengthwise. Remove the yolks and reserve the whites arranged on a dish (or a deviled egg plate—a Southern must).

Put the yolks in a small bowl with the mayonnaise, crabmeat, mustard, chili powder, and ¼ teaspoon pimentón. Season with salt and pepper and mash them together with a fork until smooth. Gently spoon a bit of the yolk mixture back into each of the whites. (You can be fancy and pipe the yolks in with a pastry bag.) Cover with plastic wrap and refrigerate for 1 hour. Sprinkle with pimentón before serving. Serve chilled.

Scallop Ceviche

serves 4 to 6

This is considered by many to be the national dish of Peru, but it is widely eaten in the Caribbean where the fish is as fresh as it gets. There are two theories of the origin of the word *ceviche*, which is also written *cerviche* or *cerbiche*. Some feel that it goes back to the Incan tradition of eating salted fish or fish marinated in *chicha* (beer) of some type. The Quechua Indian word for this dish was *sivichi*. Others feel that it has Moorish origins and takes its name from the Arabic *cibisch*. Whatever the origin, it is a simple dish and can only be made from the freshest ingredients. Don't even think about attempting this away from the seacoast. It should be eaten immediately after preparation, as the lime juice will cook the fish as soon as it is poured on and the flavor will be the best then.

1½ pounds fresh diver (bay) scallops

Salt

1 medium red onion, thinly sliced

1 red bird chile, minced

1 yellow bird chile, minced

1 cup freshly squeezed Key lime juice

Ice cubes

Place the scallops in a large nonreactive bowl. Wash them well and drain. Season with salt and add the onion and chiles. Pour the lime juice over and toss quickly. Chill the ceviche by adding a few ice cubes. Toss the mixture quickly, removing the ice cubes before they have a chance to melt. Serve immediately with toothpicks.

Marinated Green Mangos

Souskai de Mangues Verts

serves 4 to 6

There are more than sixty different varieties of mango in Martinique. In Jamaica, a local saying implies that in mango season cooks can turn over their pots and take a break, because everyone's eating their fill of the luscious fruit. There are those who do not like the taste of ripe mangoes, though, and I number myself among them. I prefer the tartness of a green mango. This salty, fiery nibble from the Indian Ocean via the French Caribbean is a perfect foil for the underlying sweetness of a 'Ti Punch (page 58).

4 medium green mangos

2 tablespoons freshly squeezed strained lime juice

1 garlic clove, minced

⅛ teaspoon minced habanero chile, or to taste

¼ cup peanut oil

Peel the mangos and cut their meat into ½-inch dice. Place them in a nonreactive bowl and mix with the lime juice, garlic, and chile. Toss until well mixed. Drizzle in the oil and toss again. Cover with plastic wrap, refrigerate, and allow to marinate for 1 to 2 hours. Serve with toothpicks.

Flaked Saltfish

Chiquetaille de Morue

serves 4 to 6

This is the French Antilles version of the dish that is a Caribbean classic. Variations are called *buljol* in Trinidad, "pick up saltfish" in Guyana and Barbados, and "Solomon Gundy" in Jamaica. It can be served with toasted French bread or crackers or incorporated into mashed ripe avocado to form *Féroce d'Avocat* (facing page).

1 pound salt cod

1 tablespoon olive oil

2 medium tomatoes, peeled, seeded, and coarsely chopped

1 small onion, minced

3 scallions, minced (including green part)

3 garlic cloves, minced

½ teaspoon fresh thyme

¼ teaspoon minced habanero chile

1½ tablespoons red wine vinegar

Crackers or toasted French bread, for serving

Desalt the cod by boiling it in water for 5 minutes, discarding the water, and boiling it again in fresh water for an additional 5 minutes. Drain the fish and flake it with your fingers, discarding any bones you may find. Place the flaked fish in a medium nonreactive bowl.

Heat the oil over medium heat in a heavy skillet. Increase the heat to high, and sauté the tomatoes, onion, scallions, garlic, thyme, and chile until the onion softens, 2 to 3 minutes. Stir in the vinegar. Pour the vegetable mixture over the flaked cod, mix well, check the seasonings, and adjust as needed. Serve immediately with crackers or toasted French bread.

Avocado and Saltfish Paste

Féroce d'Avocat

serves 4 to 6

This paste is one of the more typical appetizers in the French-speaking Caribbean. It's called *féroce* because it is usually ferociously hot with chile. You may adjust to suit your own tastebuds. Cassava meal can be found in Hispanic groceries.

2 large, ripe avocados

1 recipe Flaked Saltfish (facing page)

²/₃ cup cassava meal

Bread or crackers, for serving

Split the avocados in half lengthwise and remove the meat. Reserve the shell. Mash the avocado meat with the flaked saltfish in a bowl. Sprinkle in the cassava meal and mix. Fill the avocado shells with the mixture and serve immediately with bread or crackers.

chapter 6

Party Planner

A party should be all about inventiveness.

My mother was an inveterate party giver. She was known as the Pearl Mesta of her set (younger folks should think Oprah or any other fabulous party-giver). She inveigled her friends to dress up as babies for one fête, redressed our "finished" basement as a cabaret complete with candles in Chianti bottles for another, and in one memorable bash had them all come in tropical dress and engaged a calypso singer for a set or two. As an only child, I was allowed to sit up for the first set; I vividly remember the excitement of the drinks with maraschino cherries and pineapple spears, the frisson of excitement as the singer began to sing some more risqué songs, and the fun that was had by all.

Nothing lends itself more to a variety of party types than rum. Theme parties seem to be made for rum, with possibilities ranging from the obvious pirate party on through the more exotic New World Sacramental Wine. The only limit is your imagination and the degree to which you are wiling to challenge your friends. There are rum-tasting parties, calypso contests, and merengue dancing fetes in your future. Here are some ideas to start the parties happening.

Fête Française

This party celebrates the French side of the Caribbean and is inspired by the festivities that accompany the Fête des Cuisinières (The Feast of the Women Cooks) that is held annually on Guadeloupe around August 10, the feast day of their patron, St. Lawrence. The humor of the women is attested to by their choice of patron. St. Lawrence was martyred on the grill. In fact, the embroidered aprons that are a part of the traditional dress of the Cuisinières have a grill as their centerpiece. Each August, the ladies—the oldest of whom is over 100—get together, don their matching *grandes robes créoles*, and tons of real 18-karat gold jewelry and head off to mass followed by a grand gorge. Try one yourself in their honor. Go backward in time and look for music by old bands that play traditional *bigines*, like Alexandre Stellio who was popular in France in the 1930s. Or select your music from the albums by Kassav, the classic *zouk* group from the French Antilles.

'Ti Punch (page 58)

Pineapple-Infused Rum (page 106)

Avocado and Saltfish Paste *(Féroce d'Avocat)* **(page 149) with French bread toasts**

Marinated Green Mangos *(Souskai de Mangues Verts)* **(page 146)**

Olives

French saucissons secs (dry sausage)

A Night in Old Cuba

Whatever your thoughts about the politics of Cuba in the twentieth century, it is undeniable that the folks truly knew how to throw a party. Bars like Sloppy Joe's, La Floridita, and more welcomed thirsty travelers from the north and kept them well lubricated with daiquiris or Rum and Coca-Cola (the drink sometimes called Cuba Libre). Restaurants like the small Bodeguita del Medio offered meals of roast pork accompanied by black beans and washed down with abundant mojitos, the now-classic drink prepared with the herb known in Spanish as *yerba buena*, which is closest to our spearmint. Put some old classics like Arseno Rodriguez, Xavier Cugat, or the Buena Vista Social Club on the stereo and give yourselves a night at the Tropicana. Don't forget to include at least one version of "Babalu." So whip out your rhumba shirt and entrance your friends with:

Cuba Libre (page 77)

Daiquiris (page 65)

Mojitos (page 71)

Canchanchara (page 69)

Pumpkin Fritters with Raisins
(*Frituras de Calabaza con Pasas*)
(page 132)

Chicharrónes de cerdo (pork cracklings; buy a large bag)

SLOPPY JOE'S
HAVANA, CUBA

Merengue Madness

On Saturday night, the Malecón in Santo Domingo turns into a nonstop party. Cars parked along the wide ocean-front drive have their radios on and the graphic equalizers pump up the volume on the latest merengues. A walk down the street is like a trip to an open-air club. What began as a spontaneous expression of love of music has been transformed into a marketing opportunity, and trucks offer all manner of beverages and snacks to those for whom this stroll is the perfect way to spend a Saturday night. Create your own Malecón. Invite your neighbors and then pump up the volume; they won't complain, they'll be too busy drinking and dancing and nibbling on tropical tidbits.

Take your musical inspiration from the merengue greats, past and present. World-famous merengue singers include Cherito, Miriam Cruz & Las Chicas Del Can, Cuco Valoy, Los Toros Band, and Conjunto Quisqueya. More recent artists include Julian, Toño Rosario, Aguakate, and Amarfis. Milly Quezada is known as the Queen of Merengue. Don't forget those who made merengue popular in the United States: the Conjunto Tipico Cibaeño.

Rum Punch (page 54)

Spiced Rum (page 107)

Piña Coladas (page 82)

Dominican Fried Chicken
(Chicharrónes de Pollo) **(page 142)**

Puerto Rican Corn Fritters
(Surrulitos) **(page 136)**

New World Sacramental Wine

I've said it before and I'll say it again: rum is the sacramental wine of the New World. The African-inspired religions of the hemisphere use the sugarcane spirit to lubricate ceremonies and celebrate life. This is not really a cocktail party, but rather a celebration of rum's primal spot at the center of many New World religions. The drinks are made in the colors that are totemic for each *loa* or *orisha* (spirit) and should be sipped while listening to the music that is appropriate for each one.

Wray and Nephew 101-proof rum for Ellegua

Isle of Pines (page 93) for Ogun

A Boa Noite (page 112) for Oxum

Rum Bloody Mary (page 111) for Shango

Hurricane (page 121) for Oya

Mojito a Mi Manera (page 72) for Yemanya

Champola (page 87) for Obatala

This listing could go on and you can make your own beverages to celebrate the *orisha* and find the music to play for them. This is a ceremony, not a party. Place snifters full of rum in various spots throughout the room for the "ancestor" spirits to drink. Then put on Celia Cruz and Mercedita Valdes singing Lucumi songs. Add any recording by Cuba's Conjunto Folclorico. Switch up the drumming by Haiti's Ti Roro or add some of the music of Haiti's Vodun, then sit quietly with friends and think of the journeys that took Africa from its motherland to the New World while slowly sipping and savoring.

Pirate Party

"Arrgh!" Well shiver me timbers, why let Johnny Depp have all the fun? Sometimes getting dressed up makes for a grand time. Have your friends sign on to the good ship of fun. Send invitations in the form of treasure maps. Require costumes and have eye-patches and clip-on earrings and bandanas for the recalcitrant.

Zombies (page 124)

Navy Grogs (page 117)

Your own spiced rum (see pages 103–109)

High-Octane Limeades (page 96) made with Captain Morgan Spiced Rum

Plantain Chips (page 128)

Coconut Crisps (page 130)

Caribbean-Style Deviled Eggs (page 144)

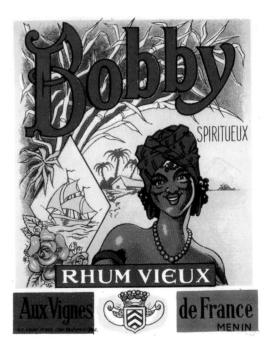

French Quarter Frolic

It's no secret that I love New Orleans. I'm one of the city's biggest boosters. This party calls on the spirit (and the spirits) of the city to ensure a grand old time. Drape your party space with purple, green, and gold (the colors of Mardi Gras). Find Mardi Gras beads online (see page 162). Then party hearty with one of the city's oldest tipples.

There are several excellent compilations of music from the Crescent City. I love *The Big Ol' Box of New Orleans* CD set for its quirky mix of the familiar and the outrageous. Search out the songs that appeal to you and create your own mix, then party like there's no tomorrow.

Hurricanes (page 121)

Rum Swizzles (page 75)

Bacon-Wrapped Pickled Watermelon (page 131)

Toasted Cashews (page 134)

Coconut Crisps (page 130)

Holiday Happening

While Caribbean cocktails mainly bring to mind tropical beaches and soft breezes, holiday season in the Caribbean has its own version of cheer. Try to bring some warmth into your holiday the Caribbean way with this festive fete.

Steel bands playing Christmas carols, Parang from Trinidad, or any one of the numerous compilations of Caribbean music are a good background for a Caribbean holiday party.

Sorrels (page 92)

Shrubbs (page 103)

Ponche Cremas (page 85)

Puerto Rican Corn Fritters *(Surrulitos)* **(page 136)**

Flaked Saltfish *(Chiquetaille de Morue)* **(page 148)**

Bacon-Wrapped Pickled Watermelon (page 131)

A is for Appleton, B is for Bacardi, C is for Curaçao

With the proliferation of rum brands and the beverage's increased popularity, it would be difficult to compile an exhaustive listing of Caribbean rums. That is something that the Web does much better, as folks can contribute from all over, with even the smallest spots getting coverage. This, then, is a general sketch in alphabetical order of some of the rums, *rhums*, and *rons* ("rum" in Spanish) that have crossed my path in the region. It's a starting point for your own tasting notes, to be filled in as you travel and as you sip.

A
Angostura (Trinidad)
Appleton (Jamaica)

B
Bacardi (Puerto Rico)
Barbancourt (Haiti)
Barcelo (Dominican Republic)
Bermudez (Dominican Republic)
Rhum Bielle (Marie Galante)
Rhum Bologne (Guadeloupe)
Bounty (St. Lucia)
Brugal (Dominican Republic)

C
Cacique (Venezuela)
Captain Morgan (Puerto Rico)
Cavalier (Antigua)
Centenario (Costa Rica)
Rhum Clement (Martinique)
Cockspur (Barbados)
Cruzan (U.S. Virgin Islands)
CSR (St. Kitt's)
Curaçao (Curaçao)

D
Rhum Damoiseau (Guadeloupe)
Demerara Distillers (Guyana)
Rhum Depaz (Martinique)
Rhum Dillon (Martinique)
Don Q (Puerto Rico)
Doorly's (Barbados)

E
El Dorado (Guyana)
ESA Fields (Barbados)

F
Flor de Cana (Nicaragua)

G
Goslings Black Seal (Bermuda)

H
Havana Club (Cuba)

J
Jack Iron (Carriacou)

L

Rhum le Maulny (Martinique)

M

Matusalem (Puerto Rico)
Montebello (Guadeloupe)
Mount Gay (Barbados)
Myers's (Jamaica)

N

Rhum Negrita (Martinique)
NOLA (New Orleans)

O

Ocumare (Venezuela)
Old Brigand (Barbados)
Old New Orleans (United States)
Old Oak (Trinidad and Tobago)

P

Père Labat (Marie Galante)
Pusser's (Trinidad)

R

Ronrico (Puerto Rico)

S

Sangster's (Jamaica)
Rhum St. James (Martinique)

T

Tia Maria (Jamaica)
Trois-Rivières (Martinique)

V

Vat 19 (Trinidad)

W

Wray and Nephew Overproof (Jamaica)

Z

Zacapa 23 (Guatemala)

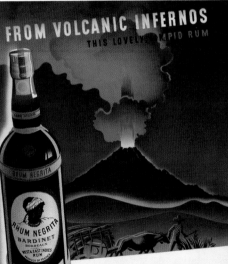

Equipment and Ingredients

Bar Tools
www.ACityDiscounts.com
www.barproducts.com
www.squidoo.com/bartender_tools

Bitters
www.feebrothers.com
www.sazerac.com/products
spiritsandcocktails.wordpress.com

Cocktail Umbrellas
www.asianideas.com

Falernum and Orgeat
www.feebrothers.com

Flavored Syrups (Lavender and others)
us.monin.com

Ginger Syrup
www.gingerpeople.com

Mardi Gras Beads and Accessories
www.emardigrasbeads.com
www.mardigrasspot.com

Passion Fruit Syrup
www.baristaproshop.com

Steen's Cane Syrup and Cane Vinegar
www.steensyrup.com

Tropical Fruit
www.friedas.com

MAKING JUNGLE RUM, PANAMA CITY.

162

rum drinks

Raise a Glass with Me

A HIGHLY OPINIONATED LISTING OF A FEW OF MY FAVORITE RUM BARS

One of the benefits of having spent more than half of my life traveling—first as travel editor for *Essence* magazine in the 1970s, then as one of the Caribbean-section editors for *Travel Weekly* in the 1980s, and then as a culinary consultant, journalist, and cookbook author from the '90s on—is that I've got a Rolodex and a Palm Pilot full of addresses. I must confess that I've spent much of my Caribbean drinking time creating my own rum routes and drinking with friends at their homes, on their boats, and all around. I have, though, also been known to belly up to a bar once or twice. Here, in no particular order, are some of my favorite places to indulge in a glass or two of rum—my favorite liquor. Some are in the Caribbean; others are in my various ports of call around the world.

John Moore Bar

Barbados is the island on which rum probably originated and it is most certainly one of the places in the Caribbean where the beverage is celebrated. There are myriad small rum shops where locals go to "fire a few" with friends. John Moore's rum shop on the main road through the Platinum Coast is one of the spots where all congregate. It's just beyond the fire station and fish market in St. James and there, at any given time, you'll run across anyone from the prime minister to the local fishermen. Mount Gay or Cockspur are the main tipples and a Corn and Oil (white rum and falernum) is one of the ways they're consumed.

An Kan Là

Located in Abymes, Guadeloupe, right in the middle of a cane field, An Kan Là is an open-air restaurant more than a bar per se. It's also a social club of sorts for the local Abymiens, who gather to table hop and eat chicken and fish that's grilled over open fires and served with great rhum 'ti punches. Some nights, there are sessions of Gros Ka, the traditional drumming that has survived in Guadeloupe since enslavement. Occasionally on Sunday afternoons there's freshly made ice cream in tropical flavors like soursop and passion fruit, served out of antique freezers.

Tommy's

These rum shops are some of my favorite spots, since for over a decade I worked for Almond Resorts, five all-inclusive properties located in Barbados and on St. Lucia. The price of a stay at the resorts includes all beverages at the properties, so the Tommy's rum shops that are on each property offer a wide choice. You'll find traditional drinks like rum punches and planter's punches, as well as a series of drinks created just for the properties by Tommy Gibson, the master mixologist who inspired the shops and oversees them.

La Rhumerie

All Caribbean bars are not located in the islands; this Parisian spot has been located on the Boulevard St. Germain since before I was a student on junior year abroad and many, many moons have passed since then. It's the place in the City of Lights to meet some Antillean friends while hoisting a punch vieux and listening to old-fashioned *biguines* or up-to-the-minute *zouk*. It's a friendly place on a cold Parisian night and always seems to convey the warmth of the Caribbean region, although that may just be the glow that the rhum brings.

Letzie's

This unprepossessing spot is another of the Barbadian rum shops. Located on the south coast in Oistin's, it's a fishermen's hangout. On Saturdays, if you get there early and you order quickly or know someone, you can get a taste of the pudding and souse that is the traditional weekend treat. The peppery pickle of the soused pig's feet is the perfect foil for a rum and ginger or a Mount Gay and lime.

Caribe Hilton

The Caribe Hilton was built in 1949 and signaled the beginning of a push for tourism in Puerto Rico. Sip a piña colada or two at the open-air bar where it all began.

Koal Keel

This Anguillan restaurant boasts a notable wine cellar and an assortment of rums that will keep even the most finicky drinker happy.

Capital Hill

Not quite a bar, this is more a local rumshop on St. Lucia. It's located high in the hills overlooking Morgan's Bay. The genial barkeep and owner has laid on many a spread for friends of mine who stop there to watch the sun go down and decompress after a day's work.

Oloffson Haiti

This white gingerbread hotel on the hills outside of Port-au-Prince would make Edward Gorey smile. It was the spot in the region where I first had my taste of the great Rhum Barbancourt and one that will always remind me of the sophistication that was Haitian life in those long-gone days. Few travelers go to Haiti these days, but those who do shouldn't miss a stop at the hotel's bar, if it's still open. It's the spot to catch up on news and to see what the world was like in another time.

Cantina de Lua

Salvador da Bahia is one of my favorite cities in the world. While it's not a place to journey for rum, the country cousin, cachaça, is pre-eminent here. I found the Cantina de Lua on one of my early trips to the city. In fact, it is mentioned in the works of writer Jorge Amado. Whippet thin and always dressed in white, owner Clarindo Silva is a notable local; in the old days he would read poetry over a loudspeaker to the folks at the bar and to those assembled in the Square every evening at midnight. Bahia has been gentrified from the old funky days when Jorge Amado inspirations lingered on each street corner and Afro-Bahian carnival groups called *afoxe* could be heard rehearsing nightly, but if I'm in the city, I'm sure to make a stop or two at the Cantina de Lua for caipirinhas and wonderful madness.

Zafra

This bar in Hoboken, New Jersey, brings a Caribbean breeze to the city that is better known for Frank Sinatra. Owner Maricel Presilla has seen to it that her bartenders celebrate her Cuban heritage with excellent mojitos and wonderful daiquiris as well as original rum cocktails.

Index